The Romantic Heritage of Marxism

Cover vignette of Mohonk mountain silhouette
courtesy of the Publications Office, State
University College, New Paltz, New York.

Studies in Modern German Literature

Peter D. G. Brown
General Editor

Vol. 15

PETER LANG
New York · Bern · Frankfurt am Main · Paris

Boria Sax

The Romantic Heritage
of Marxism

A Study
of East German
Love Poetry

PETER LANG

New York · Bern · Frankfurt am Main · Paris

Library of Congress Cataloging-in-Publication Data

Sax, Boria.
The romantic heritage of Marxism.

(Studies in modern German literature ;
vol. 15)
Bibliography: p.
Includes index.
1. Love poetry, German—Germany (East)—History and
criticism.   2. German poetry—20th century—History and
criticism.   3. Romanticism in literature.   4. Socialism
and literature—Germany (East)   5. Communism and
literature—Germany (East)   I. Title.   II. Series.
PT3720.S29   1987   801′.914′09354   87-4046
ISBN 0-8204-0487-X
ISSN 0888-3904

CIP-Kurztitelaufnahme der Deutschen Bibliothek

Sax, Boria:
The romantic heritage of marxism : a study of
East German love poetry / Boria Sax. − New
York; Bern; Frankfurt am Main; Paris: Lang,
1987.
   (Studies in Modern German Literature; Vol. 15)
   ISBN 0-8204-0487-X

NE: GT

322856

Printed by Weihert-Druck GmbH, Darmstadt, West Germany

for

Linda

ACKNOWLEDGMENTS

Professors Peter Heller, David Richards, Ronald Hauser, William Sylvester, Peter Beicken, Peter D. G. Brown and Wilma Iggers have all read parts of this manuscript at various stages of its composition and offered their suggestions. Brett Rutherford and Bruce Kelly provided valuable guidance concerning the mechanics of preparing the manuscript for publication. Kevin Doherty drafted the index. A highly abridged version of Chapter V has been published in Issue #4 of <u>GDR Monitor</u> (1982) under the title "Figures of Love: Remarks on The Poetry of Georg Maurer."

A Girl Reading (after a painting by Peter de Hooch)
German Etching from the workshops of L. H. Payne, Dresden and
    Leipzig

TABLE OF CONTENTS

INTRODUCTION

The number of motifs which are capable of arousing an intense emotional reaction in people is very limited. These include war, murder, birth of a child and religious devotion. In the Occidental world, erotic love has probably been foremost of these motifs. This becomes apparent from a casual survey of the works that are universally regarded as most important. It is more or less central to nearly all of them. One thinks of The Iliad, The Divine Comedy, the sonnets of Petrarch and most of Shakespeare.

As might be expected, a theme that has the power to stir such intense reactions has not been received in an unequivocal way. Accustomed to highly sentimental treatment of this motif, we easily forget that it has been looked upon with suspicion throughout most of history. Like any other form of intense devotion, it can easily become a socially disruptive force. Like any other elevated ideal, it is open to abuse. In German literature there are only two comparatively brief periods in which the theme of erotic love has been regularly cultivated. The first was the age of the minnesingers and the medieval epics, approximately 1150 to 1250 A.D. For many centuries thereafter, it was treated only sporadically. The second period is somewhat more difficult to date. It was foreshadowed by such poets as Günther and Fleming, reached its culmination in the work of Goethe, Hölderlin and Mörike, and has faded only gradually. Let us, for the purpose of convenience, somewhat arbitrarily assign it the period of approximately 1750 to 1950. The legacy of this period continues today primarily in popular culture, where sentimental songs provide a celebration of love that has largely vanished from poetry. It also continues in a number of isolated poems, frequently with the distancing effect of irony.

The love lyrics written in East Germany over the past two decades have been attempts to mediate between two opposing tendencies. On the one hand, there is a tendency to regard love as the source of salvation, to confront it with the greatest seriousness. This is the legacy of German Romanticism, which has, to an extent, been carried over into the Marxist tradition. On the other hand, there is pressure to subordinate personal concerns, including love, to collective priorities. East German authors have, as I will attempt to show, been compelled to deal with the tension between these contradictory expectations. Their lyrics are mostly uneasy compromises, but none has fully resolved the problem.

The criticism and scholarship of GDR (German Democratic Republic or "East German") literature are still in their infancy. The study of this literature was largely neglected in the West until the early seventies. Although an appreciable quantity of material has now been written, no real tradition of such criticism yet exists. At this time, one may speak of opposing "attitudes" or "perspectives" but hardly of "opposing theories." Each critical work must, to a large extent, make a new beginning. It must develop an original analytic framework with which the texts are to be approached.

This comparative novelty can lend excitement to a discussion like the present one. East German literature remains a comparatively unexplored territory. A certain amount of theoretical boldness which, in many areas of scholarly endeavor, would be considered presumptuous becomes virtually essential if one is to discuss GDR literature at all. Most criticism of GDR literature has a sort of tentative quality. Critics are still struggling, sometimes awkwardly, to articulate the questions which they wish to address. Such a field is well suited as a testing ground for new methodological approaches.

Several scholars, of course, are able to avoid the need for any comprehensive analytic framework by narrowing the focus of their discussion. One will therefore find a great many short articles that discuss in isolation a specific aspect of a particular artist's work. These are to be found above all in the British journal GDR Monitor (published through 1983) and the French Connaissance de la RDA. Research throughout the world is summarized in the American GDR Bulletin, a scholarly newsletter devoted primarily to reviews. Interestingly, there does not seem to be a comparable scholarly journal in West Germany. A greater emotional involvement with the subject may impede scholarly investigation. Of great importance, however, are journals such as Tintenfisch, published in West Berlin, which provides a forum for an ongoing dialogue between authors of the two German states.

As the GDR becomes increasingly established as a distinct nation, the passions that once inhibited GDR studies in West Germany have begun to cool. Since the early eighties, the Karl-Arnold Foundation, for example, has actively supported study of the GDR. This institution sponsors conferences on East Germany every December in Bonn, the proceedings of have been published in Jahrbuch zur Literatur in der DDR since 1980.

As to more comprehensive surveys of East German literature, a handful of books seem to be emerging as relatively important texts. In the GDR itself, rather few extensive discussions of GDR literature have been published. This is probably an indirect effect of political restrictions. When an author, for example, emigrates to West Germany, as so many in the last decade have done, his books will usually be removed from the shelves in stores and libraries. An attempt will be made to minimize or deny his influence. A literary history in which he is featured too prominently will suddenly start to become anachronistic. Writing under such conditions, it is extremely difficult for a scholar to trace any continuous development.

Of the literary histories that have been produced in the GDR, Eva and Hans Kaufmann's Erwartung und Angebot, a work that will sometimes be cited in this text, is perhaps the best known. The Kaufmanns, like most critics writing in the GDR, will be regarded with suspicion by most Westerners because of the blatantly propagandistic passages that are widely scattered throughout their book. It is true that the Kaufmanns do not always favor overtly propagandistic works. Political criteria are combined with aesthetic ones, often with a certain amount of subtlety, though the partisan intent is unmistakable.

A comparable bias, against against the political system of the GDR, is found in some Western books. In East German Literature by Theodore Huebener writers seem to be judged to a large extent on the basis of their opposition to the state. Such studies have tended to irritate the truly oppositional writers in the GDR. They often feel that Western critics, like their own authorities, refuse to take them seriously as artists. Sophisticated critics will de-emphasize political criteria in their evaluations, but the question of a bias, however subtle and refined, remains. Peter Demetz, in his discussion of East German authors in Post War German Literature: A Critical Introduction, devotes more space to strictly aesthetic matters, but he never neglects to mention a writer's political stance. One sometimes wonders if the charged atmosphere surrounding GDR literature prevents him from probing it too closely. He makes no attempt to come to grips with the real historical and psychological dynamics of East German literature and his discussion does not get very far beyond being a sort of textbook survey.

The most important pioneering studies of GDR literature are Fritz J. Raddatz's Traditionen und Tendenzen: Materialien zur Literatur der DDR and Hans-Dietrich Sander's Geschichte der schönen Literatur der DDR: Ein Grundriß. Both of these books suffer from some of the problems which are almost inevitable in charting unexplored territory. Attempting to synthesize vast amounts of heterogeneous information, they are only partly successful. The authors frequently appear to ramble.

All of the Western books that I have mentioned so far take a highly critical view of the social system of the GDR. Attempts to correct this alleged bias were frequently made during the seventies in the pages of the journal New German Critique, most especially in the special issue on the GDR (issue #2) published in spring of 1974. Produced with the avowed purpose of avoiding both apologetics for the GDR and legitimation of anti-Communism, the issue attempts to criticize the country and its literature from within a Marxist framework. Generally, the authors represented in the issue tend to agree with critics like Raddatz and Sander concerning the sterility of most officially sanctioned literature, but they take a basically affirmative view of the ideology on which it is based. As a result, they are constantly confronted with the awkward question of why a supposedly superior methodology has not been more productive.

This brings us to a difficulty encountered in almost all Western discussions of GDR literature. We are accustomed in the West to a relatively complete separation of literature and politics. These two are so intimately connected in East Germany that it becomes virtually impossible to discuss the former in isolation. It is difficult for Western critics writing about the GDR to maintain the sort of aloofness which is generally understood as the mark of scholarly objectivity. Attempts to depoliticize the literature preclude any close examination of its historical context. Unable to appear neutral and uneasy about being partisan, some critics in the West have approached GDR literature hesitantly if at all.

The book on GDR literature which is methodologically closest to my own is _Poetry in East Germany: Adjustments, Visions and Provocations_ by John Flores. The author is able to establish a certain objectivity by focusing on specific texts which are selected as being representative. While this does not eliminate charges of a political bias, it at least provides a context in which such charges may be examined and discussed. My analysis differs from that of Flores primarily in that I have carried his methodology further. Rather than simply discussing excerpts as Flores has done, I have examined entire poems. I have also analyzed them at greater length.

What I propose is to view poetry as a projective technique by which an author will necessarily reveal far more about his own fears, hopes and prejudices than he or she ever intends. This is done partly by means of the associations which the imagery suggests. Much is revealed through a poem's dramatic structure. The point at which the climax is reached, if the poem contains one at all, will probably be something of special importance to the author. A writer will also betray a great deal by means of rhythms. When these appear too smooth and mechanical, we may doubt his sincerity. If the rhythmic pattern breaks down, we may identify an area of crisis and uncertainty. The repeated use or avoidance of certain words can also tell us about the author of a poem. Similarly, the reception of a poetic work can tell us about the spiritual climate in which it appears. When, for example, a critic projects certain values into a poem, that will indicate his priorities and, thereby, the prevailing mood in the country where he writes.

There may be some affinity between my approach and the sort of close analysis most strongly identified with William Empson and his book Seven Types of Ambiguity, fashionable in the early sixties but now less often employed. The fundamental difference is that Empson uses close analysis in an attempt to explain the aesthetic effect of a work. I am, for the purpose of this discussion, somewhat less interested in the artistic impact of a poem than in the attitudes it embodies. An overly exclusive emphasis on form and aesthetics can, I believe, too often obscure the content of a literary work. A similar sort of analysis has long been applied to paintings but seldom to literature.

My method could also be compared to a psychoanalytic approach, but, here again, I think there are fundamental differences. For one thing, I prefer to avoid technical terminologies and use only the language of common sense. Still more significantly, I am not trying to probe the innermost recesses of an author's psyche, merely to establish his or her attitudes with respect to certain rather clearly defined topics. Because the theme of love is so emotionally charged, I believe it will be well suited to this sort of analysis. Where feelings run deep, it is especially difficult for rationalizations, in particular those which are ideologically motivated, to obscure them.

The implications of the discussion here will go far beyond the confines of the selected topic. Furthermore, the method could, I am convinced, easily be extended to the study of other literary and cultural themes. To an extent I have adopted it here not only to the discussion of poets but of philosophers such as Marx and Lenin. I have focused on their use of language in selected passages.

I have tried to select authors for this discussion whose work is in some way representative. My list corresponds only roughly to a selection of the most celebrated poets in the country. Peter Huchel, Johannes Bobrowski, Erich Arendt and Reiner Kunze may be equal in stature to the poets here discussed, but their work is less typical.

All translations in this book are my own unless otherwise indicated. I have tried to stay close to the originals, but not at the price of artistic quality. A translator, like an author, is most effective if he recognizes the limits imposed by the language in which he works. A fanatical adherence to the letter of the original is, in fact, no fidelity at all. There will be times when the discussion in these pages involves a close reading of the poems and will only be fully understood by reference to the original texts. These have been included with all passages of poetry, though not with prose.

What, above all, has attracted me to the study of East German writing is the comparative seriousness with which the literary vocation is regarded in that part of the world. Even the restrictions experienced by dissident writers suggest a certain respect for their power. A sort of primitive magic still seems to reside in the printed word. Authors in countries like West Germany and the United States may pity their East European colleagues who must contend with a far greater degree of censorship, yet that pity is usually mixed with a trace of envy.

For all the difficulties they may contend with, writers in the East probably have a greater influence on the societies in which they live. They tend to be viewed as cultural guardians. Much as I treasure the freedom of expression granted to me as a citizen of the United States, I am concerned that we have become accustomed to a highly trivialized view of literature and the arts. Perhaps contact with the culture of Eastern and Central Europe may help us to overcome this. It is largely out of such a hope that this book has been written.

CHAPTER I

THE ROMANTIC HERITAGE OF
MARXISM IN EAST
GERMANY

The theoretical work of Marx contains very little discussion of relations between the sexes[1] and no substantial discussion of erotic love. The many who have looked to him for guidance in these areas have found only a handful of passages widely scattered throughout his voluminous work. These tend to be highly abstract, ambiguous and often no longer than a few brief sentences. There is no reason to believe that Marx himself attached much importance to these passages, yet they receive much attention simply because there is nothing else. The omission itself is significant. For a philosopher who created such an extraordinarily comprehensive intellectual system, the comparative silence on such a fundamental aspect of human experience requires some explanation. This silence is particularly striking when one considers the prominent role played by sexuality in most of the traditions from which Marx drew his inspiration.

Sexuality figures importantly in the work of other Socialist thinkers, although in highly contrasting ways. Fourier viewed sexual repression as a major cause of social and political evils and wished to do away with almost all restraints. Proudhon, on the other hand, emphasized the family as the basic unit of society and wished to safeguard it by means of a highly conservative morality.[2] Although the few passages in which Marx does discuss sexuality show, as we shall see, traces of both the conservative and libertarian ideals, no attempt to reconcile these is made. As a result, this highly ambivalent heritage has remained with the Socialist movement to this day.

Leszek Kolakowski views the silence on the theme of sexuality as part of a larger pattern: "Marx's ignoring of the body, physical death, sex and aggression, geography and human fertility--all of which he turns into purely social realities--is one of the most characteristic yet most neglected features of his utopia."[3] Marx, to put it another way, tends to disregard all factors which set limits to human endeavor. Sexuality, associated with the body and thereby with human frailty and mortality, plays no significant role in his work. There is a tendency to regard a human being as a sort of disembodied consciousness, probably due to Marx's heritage in the tradition of German Idealism.

This may explain not only the paucity of Marx's discussion but also its unsystematic character. Sexuality is not regarded as a given. It is not viewed as a limitation with which we must live but rather as a social creation. There seemed no need to reconcile contradictions, as these, in any case, were expected to be resolved in the course of historical evolution.

The few times that Marx does touch on relationships between the sexes in his theoretical work, he does not seem to recognize love as an autonomous social or historical factor. Sexual relationships, at least as they have existed throughout history, are reduced to an economic basis. Criticizing a certain sort of thoughtless Communism in his Economic and Philosophical Manuscripts of 1844, Marx compares this to the movement from marriage—in his view "a form of exclusive private property"—to a "community of women." Woman becomes "a piece of communal property," but the essential exploitative relationship is not abolished.[4]

He goes on to say that the relationship of man to woman illustrates the way a social relationship takes on the aspect of a natural function. What we think of as "human nature," in other words, turns out to be socially conditioned.[5] A corollary would seem to be that sexuality, and the whole range of feelings associated with it, will change with the broader structure of society.

In The German Ideology there is a frequently quoted passage in which Marx views the earliest social structures as an extension of the the patriarchal family: "...slavery latent in the family, though still very crude, is the first property, but even at this early stage it corresponds perfectly to the definition of modern economists who call it the power of disposing of the labor-power of others."[6] This rather fragmentary idea, however, is not developed by Marx.

In their Manifesto of the Communist Party, Marx and Engels give a striking statement of their views:

But you Communists would introduce community of women, screams the whole bourgeoisie in chorus.

The bourgeois sees in his wife a mere instrument of production. He hears that the instruments of production are to be exploited in common, and, naturally, can come to no other conclusion than that the lot of being common to all will likewise fall to women.

He has not even a suspicion that the real point aimed at is to do away with the status of women as mere instruments of production.

For the rest, nothing is more ridiculous than the virtuous indignation of our bourgeois at the community of women which, they pretend, is to be openly and officially established by the Communists. The Communists have no need to introduce community of women; it has existed almost from time immemorial.

Our bourgeois, not content with having the wives and daughters of the proletarians at their disposal, not to speak of common prostitutes, take the greatest pleasure in seducing each other's wives.

Bourgeois marriage is in reality a system of wives in common and thus, at the most, what the Communists might possibly be reproached with is that they desire to introduce, in substitution for a hypocritically concealed, an openly legalized community of women. For the rest, it is self-evident that the abolition of the present system of production must bring with it the abolition of the community of women springing from that system, i.e., of prostitution both public and private.7

The rhetorical power of this passage can almost make us neglect to notice that the authors have not really answered the charge. Do the Communists intend to establish (or perpetuate) a community of women? Marx and Engels have merely responded ad hominem, turning the charge around and accusing the bourgeoisie of "a system of wives in common." The passage is profoundly ambiguous.

Both the sexual morality and the license of the bourgeoisie are condemned, but nothing is said of what would take their place. Marx and Engels apparently thought that this would be answered in the course of historical evolution, that a change in productive relationships would create new sexual patterns that could not yet be foreseen. Characteristically, they have nothing to say about the actual nature of the future society, yet the question which they here decline to answer has haunted the Socialist movement ever since. The ambivalence in the attitude expressed towards sexuality has placed subsequent Communists in something of a quandary. Since both strict morality and libertinism seem to be, in the context of existing productive relationships, rejected as bourgeois, what attitude is to be adopted while we are waiting for the Communistic society to emerge? On this question as well, Marx and Engels do not offer us any guidance. In the early stages of the movement, the question did not seem to be of major importance. As it has become increasingly apparent that a utopia is not imminent, that mankind must at least be prepared for an extended wait, this issue has grown more difficult to evade.

The later works of Marx contain even less material of importance on sexual questions. Of some note is a remark in a letter to Kugelmann (December 12, 1868) to the effect that the degree of progress in any society may be measured exactly by the degree to which women in that society are emancipated.[8] This idea, however, is neither supported nor elaborated upon.

I would now like to examine Marxism as an offshoot and continuation of the Romantic tradition. The idea may at first seem paradoxical, as Marxists have generally regarded Romanticism with hostility and contempt. They tend to see it as an ideology of escapism, a refusal to recognize social realities. At times Marxists have almost seemed to define themselves by their opposition to Romanticism, yet one can discern an element of filial rebellion in the vehemence of their repudiation.

"Romanticism" is a notoriously ambiguous term which I prefer not to use without a few words of explanation. It refers to a movement throughout Europe in the later eighteenth and the nineteenth centuries, corresponding roughly with the start of the Industrial Revolution. Beyond their point of departure, the Romantics had very little in common. All reacted against the supposed "progress" which was taking place around them. They lamented the growth of industry as destruction of the natural world, the rise of a commerce as a fragmentation of society. Starting from this negative critique, they reached greatly differing conclusions. They ranged from political radicals to extreme conservatives, from atheists to orthodox Catholics.

The Romantics opposed the prosaic world around them with a vision of primal harmony. A few such as Baudelaire sought this simply in the world of imagination or, like Wordsworth, in the natural world, but the majority identified it with a period in the past. For Rousseau, often regarded as the father of Romanticism, this was a "state of nature" before the advent of civilization. For important British Romantics--most notably Shelly, Byron and Keats--the time of harmony was Classical Greece. For another contingent of British Romantics, including Carlyle and Scott, as well as for Hugo in France, it was identified with the Middle Ages.

In most of Northern Europe, the Romantics stood in defiant opposition to their times. Only in Germany did Romanticism become the dominant cultural trend. Germany lagged behind in industrial development and the aesthetic critique of modernity was re-enforced by nationalistic sentiments. The British and French Romantics tended to form relatively circumscribed groups, set apart from the rest of society. In Germany Romanticism formed a fairly cohesive ideological movement.

The German Romantics idealized the Middle Ages. Their poetry was filled with nostalgic images of ruined castles in the forest, as well as medieval motifs such as knights, kings, dragons and wandering minstrels. The originally rebellious impulse behind Romanticism took a conservative turn. The fragmentation characteristic of industrial society was contrasted with the feudal order and its simple faith. Novalis, Friedrich Schlegel and Brentano converted to Catholicism, while Eichendorff persisted in it throughout his life.

The Romantics were absolute in their demands, condemning the world for not living up to these. Forced to live in a reality that did not conform to their dreams, they were plagued by melancholy and discontent. The constant intrusion of prosaic reality was treated with defiance, sometimes tempered--as with Hoffmann and Heine--by humor. A few Romantics such as Wackenroder tried consciously to reject the world for the realm of art. The majority were unable to make such a choice.

If the most irreducible feature of Romanticism is indeed rebellion against the emerging industrial society--that is, against Capitalism--then Marxism belongs to that tradition. A number of other similarities suggest themselves as well. Marx provided a vision of harmony that was even vaguer, and thereby more absolute, than those of the Romantics. One of the few thinkers in the Marxist tradition who recognizes and affirms the movement's Romantic origin is Michael Löwy. A rediscovery of Romanticism, he believes, could restore to Marxism some of the revolutionary fervor which has been lost through overly mechanistic interpretations. He points out the debt owed by Marx and Engels to such Romantic thinkers as Carlyle and Balzac for their critique of Capitalism.[9]

Löwy emphasizes Marx's roots in the broader European tradition, yet if we go back to Marx's student days we find him
writing poetry directly in the German tradition of Romanticism.
All of the trademarks are there: the knights, fairies, minstrels
and damsels, the melancholy, the sentimentalism, the longing for
the absolute. One cannot simply attribute this to the prevailing
fashion. The Romantic movement had receded by this time and the
style was already anachronistic. The reason must, therefore, be
sought in Marx's character.

Repudiated by Marx shortly after their composition, the
poems have consistently been ignored. It is interesting to note
that even in the GDR, where great importance is sometimes
attached to the master's casual remarks, the poems are never
anthologized. This is probably unfortunate. Though clumsily
written, the poems are not without a certain power. Of far more
importance, however, than their aesthetic appeal is the insight
they provide into Marx's character. They are the work of a young
man, still comparatively naive, who has not yet learned to
rationalize his feelings, employing the most personal of artistic
forms. One of the few to have recognized this is Edmund Wilson,
who says the poetry "is of interest in presenting the whole
repertoire of his (Marx's) characteristic impulses and emotions
before they are harnessed to the pistons of his system." Wilson
adds that "the lyrics have something of the hard and dark
crystallization which is afterward to distinguish Marx's writing,
and they leave in the mind of the reader certain recurrent
symbols."10

The poems show us a Marx who, superficially at least, is the
very opposite of the man whom most people, whether they accept
his ideas or not, are used to imagining. If the author of Capital
is present in these poems, it is in the harsh sound which contrasts oddly with the poetic content. Far from being lyrical,

their music chimes along mechanically from line to line. In this respect, the poems suggest a temperament that is not ecstatic but plodding and determined. This poetic insufficiency in Marx's work would later, used more consciously, be transformed into his greatest stylistic strength. This tension between the Romantic imagery and a prosaic sound foreshadows the sarcasm which is so often impressive in his prose. The Romantic sympathies would later be overwhelmed by the prosaic undertone.

Leonard P. Wessel Jr. has gone so far as to use the early poems as a basis for a reinterpretation of Marx's entire work. In his book Karl Marx, Romantic Irony and the Proletariat: The Mythopoetic Origins of Marxism, Wessel argues that Marxism is not a scientific system at all but an aesthetic vision rendered through a technical-sounding terminology. Marxism, he maintains, has roots in the work of Romantics such as Friedrich Schlegel, whose lectures were attended by Marx as a young man. To the unpoetic and demythologized view of nature provided by the emerging sciences, German Romantics such as Schlegel and Novalis opposed another reality, animated by an all-pervasive spirit. For Schlegel, this found expression as "Romantic irony," a mode in which nothing is ever allowed to become fixed or objectified. All was to remain forever fluid, ambiguous and many-faceted. The Marxian adaptation of Hegelian dialectics, locating the dialectical process in reality rather than in ideas, was, according to Wessel, nothing but "irony made flesh."[11] Marxism followed the Romantic tradition in identifying the de-poeticized reality with the bourgeoisie.[12] The Romantic hero, embodiment of the forces which oppose objectification, was, Wessel believes, merely replaced by the proletariat. The artistic appeal of this vision explains, in his opinion, the strong hold that Marxism has exerted over the imagination despite a general failure of its prophecies.

Wessel supports his view with an examination of Marx's early literary endeavors. He points out that despite their Romantic character, the poems which Marx wrote completely fail to evoke the sort of magical atmosphere that is found in the work of major Romantic poets. He views Marx's theoretical writing as another attempt to execute the project which Marx first conceived as a Romantic poet--the poeticization of all reality. This is only a brief summary of Wessel's rather intricate analysis. Whether we accept all of it or not, it can at least direct us to generic and historical ties between Romanticism and Marxism.

A number of important ideas in both of these two movements may be traced to Christianity. Like Christianity, Romanticism and Marxism find expression in apocalyptic images relating to a final struggle between good and evil. All three movements share a concern with the poor and disadvantaged, whom they attempt, in various ways, to help and, sometimes, to glorify. With respect to literature, Wessel's theory would help explain why the traditions of German Romanticism have been far more cultivated in the GDR than in the Federal Republic. Characteristic Romantic forms such as the folk song and the fairy tale are, for example, far more frequently employed in the former country.

Marx differed from the German Romantics in his respect for technology, but, even more fundamentally, in his optimism. Like the Romantics, he recognized the damage which attended the process of industrialization. He believed, nevertheless, that it represented progress for mankind. He shared the limitless aspiration, the longing for the absolute, that is characteristic of Romanticism. Unlike the Romantics, he claimed to have dis-covered a method by which such aspiration could actually be achieved. He, therefore, located his vision of ultimate harmony in the indefinite future rather than in the misty past. This is the "Promethean" spirit, which, as Wessel has pointed out, is already starting to emerge in some of his later poems.

I would like, at this point, to return to the theme of erotic love. Both Romanticism and Marxism derive from Christianity the idea of love as a redeeming power. The divine love in Christianity is eroticized in Romanticism. In Marxism it is secularized and qualified, becoming solidarity within the proletariat.

It is true that even in the few discussions of sexual questions that are found in the theoretical work of Marx, love does not play a significant role. Salvation through love is, however, a primary theme in his early poetry. His poems suggest the uncharted location of sexual love in the complex of interconnected feelings, ideas and aspirations that are identified with the name of Marx today. Take the closing stanzas of the poem "Menschenstoltz," dedicated to his wife Jenny:

Jenny! Darf ich kühn es sagen,
  Daß die Seelen liebend wir getauscht,
Daß in eins sie glühend schlagen,
  Daß ein Strom durch ihre Wellen rauscht,

Dann werf' ich den Handschuh höhnend
  Einer Welt ins breite Angesicht,
Und die Riesenzwergin stürzte stöhnend,
  Meine Glut erdrückt ihr Trümmer nicht.

Götterähnlich darf ich wandeln,
  Siegreich ziehn durch ihr Ruinenreich,
Jedes Wort ist Gluth und Handeln,
  Meine Brust dem Schöpferbusen gleich.

Jenny! May I boldly say it,
  That we have lovingly exchanged souls,
That they beat glowingly as one.
  That a stream roars through their waves.

Then I'll hurl the glove scornfully
  Into the world's broad countenance,
And let the gigantic she-dwarf plunge with groans.
  Her debris will not crush my glow.

Similar to gods I dare roam,
  March triumphantly through the realm of ruins;
Every word is flame and acting,
  My breast equal to the Creator's bosom.13
                    (translated by L. P. Wessel Jr.)

In the last two stanzas we recognize an unbounded confidence in the ability of man to defy fate and to change the world. Rather than simply longing for the absolute, Marx is now ready to demand it. The existing order is no longer viewed with sadness. It is viewed with contempt. We can even discern here the emerging outlines of Marx's theoretical system. What Marx says here is that love has inspired him, showing that man can be equal to God. The union of two souls in love is later to be replaced by the joining of countless souls--the proletariat.

If this poem is, however awkward and immature, a fairly honest record of Marx's feelings, it may indicate how the unmentioned theme of erotic love is silently implicit in Marx's later work, perhaps through the intensity with which his demands are formulated. What we have is a love that is first idealized, then later sublimated in the task of building a new society. This is a pattern that we will encounter repeatedly in love lyrics of the GDR.

It is fortunate for the Socialist world that Marx did not say more about the theme of sexual love. Any more comprehensive statement would almost certainly have been abused. As Marx's work was elevated to the status of scripture and even casual statements were quoted as a final authority, this intimate realm remained untouched, retaining a sort of sanctity. Marx's impact here is primarily through his silence on the theme, not through anything he said.

Insofar as one may speak at all of a Communist tradition with respect to love and sex, it is an unsystematic blend of the radical, the conservative and the commonplace. Marx himself left only a number of isolated hints, observations and suggestions but no consistent method of approach. In examining the subsequent development of the Marxist tradition, we find a vast amount of peripheral material but no really central texts. The theme of erotic love tends to be treated in connection with the more central topic of female emancipation, though this as well is not among the movement's most central concerns.

As the Marxist tradition developed, its Romantic heritage found continued expression as the tendency to see things in terms of absolutes, something that is generally characteristic of both social radicals and conservatives. Perhaps the most significant text on sexual questions within the Marxist tradition is Engels' The Origin of the Family and the State. Drawing heavily on the work of the American anthropologist Lewis Morgan, who studied among the Iroquois Indians, Engels formulated a history of sexual mores which I will summarize briefly. Starting from a primeval period of indiscriminate promiscuity, human society developed by progressively limiting the number of people from among whom sexual partners could be chosen. Eventually this produced the matriarchal gens, a sort of tribe or family within which sexual intercourse was forbidden. With the discovery of fatherhood, women were overthrown and the patriarchy began. Monogamy developed in Roman times, not as an expression of love but to facilitate the patrilineal inheritance by guaranteeing the male line. Sexual love, Engels claims, did not exist until the German middle ages, where the institution of monogamy was combined with the Teutonic tradition of respect for women. The first historical expressions of sexual love were not within the context of marriage but rather the adulterous "songs of dawn" in which a man takes leave of his mistress. In modern times bourgeios marriage continues to be essentially a monetary contract. Only among the proletariat, whose impoverishment does not permit property to become a social factor, does marriage based on love actually exist. The Origin of the Family and the State is the most speculative and perhaps even the most ambitious of the Marxist classics. Based as it is on material collected by Morgan which is now regarded as highly dubious[14], it is, even in Socialist countries, less canonical than, say, Marx's Capital. Our concern here is, however, less with its validity than with the attitudes it reveals. In contrast to other Socialists such as Saint-Simone and Fourier, Engels shows little interest in the emancipation of the flesh. Sexuality is always viewed either as an expression of love or as a link in a network of economic institutions. He speaks of sodomy as an "abominable practice" and adds that the Greeks degraded both their gods and themselves with the myth of Ganymede.[15]

It is true that Engels constantly chides the "philistines" who resist the idea that society, in the course of its evolution, went through such apparently promiscuous stages as group marriage. Nevertheless, he regards such systems, like stages in mankind's evolution from an ape-like creature, as arrangements appropriate to a certain historical period but no longer relevant today. His purpose is to discourage sentimentalism about the

past. Group marriage is said to be characteristic of "barbarism,"
monogamy of "civilization."[16] He speaks of sexual love as a
"moral advance."[17] Though he does not view the monogamous tie
as necessarily indissoluble, he contemplates its termination only
when the love which, ideally, is its foundation has died. As to
the future, Engels has this to say:

> Having risen from economic causes, will monogamy disappear
> when these causes disappear? One might answer, not without
> reason: far from disappearing, it will on the contrary begin
> to be realized completely. For with the transformation of
> the means of production into social property there will
> disappear also wage-labor, the proletariat, and therefore
> the necessity for a certain--statistically calcu-
> lable--number of women to surrender themselves for money.
> Prostitution disappears; monogamy, instead of collapsing, at
> last becomes a reality--also for men.[18]

Although Engels leaves the future somewhat open, this is the only
possibility that he contemplates.

Engels' book was essentially a theoretical work and not
intended to have any practical applications.[19] Of conceivably
greater influence was August Bebel's Women and Socialism, first
published in 1879. Unlike Engels, Bebel was primarily a pragmatic
party organizer and not a theoretician. He advocated equality of
opportunity between the sexes, believing that both men and women
should be able to choose their own professions. He, nevertheless,
also believed that certain innate differences between the sexes
with respect to both temperament and ability would do much to
determine their choices.[20] Like Marx, Bebel had nothing to say
about erotic love.

Bebel believed only in a revolution achieved by parliamentary means and declined to support the Russian revolution. Generally speaking, sexual emancipation, together with Feminism, became primarily the province of the more reformist elements within the German Social Democratic Party, ignored and even attacked by the radicals.[21] The fascination which the avantgarde has always felt for Communism has never been reciprocated. On cultural questions, the Communist movement has always tended toward a cultural conservatism, not untouched by a Romantic nostalgia. The radical theoretician Rosa Luxemburg went so far as to deny that there was a "women's problem."[22] The other preeminent female organizer around the turn of the century, Clara Zetkin, regarded Feminism as a "right deviation." She built he largest Socialist women's organization at the Second International through uncompromising attacks on "bourgeois feminists."[23]

Zetkin, however, went too far for Lenin when she had sex and marriage discussed at meetings of working women. Lenin protested that the women did not have sufficient historical knowledge for the correct sort of Marxist analysis.[24] In a passionate monologue, Lenin continued: "The decay, putrescence and filth of bourgeois marriage with its difficult dissolution, its license for the husband and bondage for the wife, and its disgustingly false sexual morality and relations fill the best and most spiritually active of people with the utmost loathing."[25] Lenin also said, however: "I was also told that sex problems are a favorite subject in your youth organizations too, and that there are hardly enough lecturers on the subject. This nonsense is especially dangerous and damaging to the youth movement. It can lead to sexual excesses, to overstimulation of sex life and to wasted health and strength of young people."[26]

Lenin's choice of words here is interesting. When he speaks of bourgeois marriage in terms of "decay, putrescence and filth," calls its morality "disgustingly" false or believes those who are "spiritually active" will respond with "utmost loathing," the scatological language suggests a discomfort with the subject that is perhaps related to prudery. Such expressions are too extreme to be explained as a mere polemic. If the institution is wrong, why should he respond with this physical revulsion rather than, say, sadness, amusement or even simple anger? This quotation from Lenin is an unusually open expression of an attitude already found in Marx and other representatives of the Communist movement--a great reluctance to deal with the theme of erotic love at all.

The Russian Revolution, like virtually all major social upheavals, brought with it a very brief period of sexual license. This won the applause of sexual liberationists such as the young Wilhelm Reich, who brought back glowing accounts of his visit to the Soviet Union. The vagueness surrounding Communist doctrine on erotic questions no doubt enabled them to project their personal dreams on to the Soviet reality. Such people, however, were quickly to be disillusioned. As the Bolsheviks consolidated their control over the country, the cultural conservatism of leaders such as Lenin quickly asserted itself. By 1945, when the Russians occupied East Germany, few traces of the old libertarian ideals remained.

The East German family law of 1966 states that the family "remains the basic unit of society." Marriage is defined as a "life-long union based on mutual love, respect and faithfulness, understanding and trust and unselfish help for each other...to give rise to the founding of a family..."[27] Pornography is forbidden in the GDR today. All social institutions are oriented toward marriage and family life. When single, young people tend to live with their parents or in hostels connected with their place of work. Only on marriage do they receive an apartment of their own. People under 26 who earn less than a fixed sum are entitled to a "marriage loan" which is cancelled out upon marriage and the birth of children.28

Nevertheless, erotic love tends to be de-emphasized. Like all personal feelings, it is to be subordinated to the task of building a new society. Even today, concern with erotic love--not altogether unlike explicit sex in the West--often has to be justified by demonstrating a larger social value. Erotic love, in brief, is viewed as a potentially disruptive force that must be channelled or contained. The theme of love was viewed with considerable suspicion for some time after the founding of the East German state. While not prohibited, it was regarded as somewhat indulgent and overly individualistic. In 1953, it was necessary for Walter Ulbricht to declare that love as well as work would now be considered a legitimate subject for films.29

The presentation of love in contemporary East German books for children is discussed by Dr. Edith Georg in an article entitled "Denkst du schon an die Liebe?", published in 1977 in the GDR periodical Neue deutsche Literatur. It is interesting to note that almost nothing in the discussion seems to derive directly from Marx, Engels or the other founders of Communism. These are hardly mentioned at all. Political categories do not play a central role in the analysis. The real foundation of the discussion is pyschological observation which, however, is based far more on common sense than on Freud or any other academic school. Georg proceeds with a survey of several books of stories for young people. She concludes that children's books touch frequently on the theme of love but that its importance is de-emphasized. Love is generally presented as part of a larger problem, not as a fundamental focus of a person's life.

Nevertheless, it tends to be treated with remarkable seriousness. A partnership is almost always presented as being permanent. Teasing and flirtation are not depicted. Sensuality, at least in its coarser forms, tends to be ignored. Georg concludes with the following paragraph:

> All in all: there is more than a beginning to be grateful for. Important foundations have been laid down. Trails have been blazed. Still to be attained remain joy in discovery, courage to examine new perspectives, increased sensibility, familiar concourse with the uncertain multitude of emotions--in a word: the love of love in children's books.[30]

The ideal is a relaxed acceptance which values love but does not dramatize it.

As one approaches the more sophisticated forms of adult literature, the ideological perspective, surprisingly, becomes more pronounced, though it still tends to be presented with a good deal of flexibility. One writer of prose who has treated the theme of love with particular persistence is Günter de Bruyn. When asked in an interview about the oppression of women in traditional love stories, he replied:

> I would be careful there. Every story of genuine love presupposes that both lovers, as you say, are subjects. And you find that already in the late antique period (think of Amor and Psyche, Daphnis and Chloe, Hero and Leander), where woman in the social reality was not only oppressed, where she was actually a slave, a prey, a possession of the man. If one wished to speak of emancipatory efforts there, one could say: every love is a sort of emancipation.[31]

Such a position is not at all unusual. The only clear restriction that one can observe consistently in the literary treatment of sexual love is that its importance, in the event of a conflict, is never allowed to overshadow social goals. The emotional power of the theme demands that it be handled with caution.

When difficulties cannot be solved, love, like other desirable things in East Germany, tends to be projected into the future. Here, as in other areas, people are encouraged to dispense with immediate gratification for the sake of a greater satisfaction to be enjoyed by future generations. In a preface to a collection of German love poems, entitled Sieben Rosen hat der Strauch, Heinz Czechowski, himself a considerable poet, expresses the view that erotic love in East Germany has already assumed a distinctively new quality:

> We know that even in our time love is not yet free from doubt and personal pain. But in the verse of Fürnberg and Becher, Brecht and Maurer, in the poems of the younger and youngest poets, there is a confidence that the happiness of lovers will be determined by an order that liberates and is liberated from want and oppression. Perhaps some reader may still miss consummation, by comparison with the classical period of German literature, in reading the most recent poems. He will find the unmistakable tones that announce a new quality in German love lyrics and, to an extent, already possess it.32

Implicit here is the expectation that all doubt and personal pain involved in love will eventually disappear.

In their preface to a collection entitled Deutsche Liebesgedichte, editors Walter Lewerenz and Helmut Preißler express similar sentiments, emphasizing the political dimension even more:

But only when poets recognize the powers that can remake our earth--in order that love can thrive--, only as new initiatives flow into literature from the free thought of the class striving forwards, only then will love in poems be fully experienced as spiritual comradeship, as the joyous or painful but always fortunate experience of free individuals. Free from the bonds of the old society, love also liberates itself from the narrow thinking of the old society, it is no longer a phrase and no longer a dream, now begins its finest hour.[33]

Since the early sixties when these collections appeared, the inflated, rhetorical style of these statements has become somewhat less usual.

In summary, we may state that erotic love is viewed in East Germany as a potentially disruptive factor and is kept in check by means of a somewhat delicate balance of forces. The extreme seriousness and idealism with which it tends to be regarded is counteracted by a low emphasis on strictly personal fulfillment. Like most things that can inspire strong emotions, it is feared but, so far as possible, also put to use.

CHAPTER II

BERTOLT BRECHT: THE EXTREME RETICENCE

The study of Brecht presents us with problems that are not often
encountered with a young literature such as that of the GDR. The
sheer quantity of work that has been written about Brecht over a
short period of time creates, of itself, certain difficulties.
Whether we actually understand Brecht any better for all of these
countless articles and books seems questionable. We no doubt have
a greater amount of factual information, but the task of syn-
thesizing this information is not greatly facilitated. For one
thing, the difficulty of encompassing the vast amounts of secondary literature can have the effect of reducing criticism, especially brief discussions like my own, to a series of specialties.
Furthermore, commentators, in responding to one another, often
tend to get further from the text itself. Intellectual myth-
ologies can be built around the text, which in the case of less
known writers do not have much opportunity to develop. It be
comes increasingly difficult to view the literature objectively.

A second, related difficulty is the extreme adulation that has been bestowed on Brecht. In the GDR he is often viewed as a model Communist. In the West, however, we find the worship of genius as the embodiment of some primordial vitality. It is somewhat ironic that Brecht, who sometimes protested and rebelled against this sort of veneration, should finally be accorded it.

What I will attempt in this chapter is to recover some objectivity by focusing closely on the texts themselves. This approach is, of course, far easier with poetry than with prose and drama, both forms in which the meaning of individual passages tends to be dependent upon a much larger context. When I cite secondary literature in this chapter, this will not always be for the intrinsic value of the arguments. Often, it will be to make this secondary literature itself and object of study, to illustrate some of the contrasting myths--ideas that find little basis in the texts themselves--that have grown up around Brecht's work.

Brecht's writing tends to be impersonal. The early ballads are narrated in the third person. The later poems may often be written in the first person, but the poet speaks as Everyman, as a sort of hypothetical observer. The later plays are written with the explicit purpose of creating psychic distance or "alienation." As we shall see in this discussion, there has been a frequent tendency for critics to project far more feeling into his poems than they actually express.

Similarly, critics have tended to see in Brecht's artistic development a confirmation of their own political views. Thus Hannah Arendt, a pro-Western critic, finds greater passion in the work Brecht wrote before emigrating to the GDR. The East German critics Klaus Schuhmann and Hans Kaufmann, on the other hand, find the work Brecht wrote after his emigration to be informed by greater humanity.

The love scenes in Brecht's plays are characterized by what Martin Esslin has called "extreme reticence."[1] More often than not, they parody popular sentimentality. The love scene between Paul and Jenny In Mahagonny takes place amid the noise of impatient customers in a brothel. The love scene between Grusche and Simon in Der kaukasische Kreidekreis is often pointed to, especially by East German critics, as evidence that Brecht had overcome his discomfort with the subject. In reality, this is very far from true. For most of the scene the couple speak to each other in the third person. Their statements have a sort of stylized formality. The characters never actually even declare their love. It is not even clear how much of Grusche's promise to remain faithful is due to love and how much to propriety and custom. As the scene ends and they depart, they do not embrace but bow deeply, almost ritualistically. This is not to deny that scene is effective. Brecht has managed to put his usual reticence to good use, suggesting modesty and reserve.

In all of Brecht's published work, there is not a single love poem addressed to a named person. The closest is "Erinnerung an Marie A.":

ERINNERUNG AN MARIE A.

1

An jenem Tag im blauen Mond September
Still unter einem jungen Pflaumenbaum
hielt ich sie, die stille bleiche Liebe
In meinem Arm wie einen holden Traum.
Und über uns im schönen Sommerhimmel
War eine Wolke, die ich lange sah
Sie war sehr weiß und ungeheuer oben
Und als ich aufsah, war sie nimmer da.

2

Seit jenem Tag sind viele, viele Monde
Geschwommen still hinunter und vorbei.
Die Pflaumenbäume sind wohl abgehauen
Und fragst du mich, was mit der Liebe sei?
So sag ich dir: ich kann mich nicht erinnern
Und doch, gewiß, ich weiß schon, was du meinst.
Doch ihr Gesicht, das weiß ich wirklich nimmer
Ich weiß nur mehr: ich küßte es dereinst.

3

Und auch den Kuß, ich hätt ihn längst vergessen
Wenn nicht die Wolke dagewesen wär
Die weiß ich noch und werd ich immer wissen
Sie war sehr weiß und kam von oben her.
Die Plaumenbäume blühn vielleicht noch immer
Und jene Frau hat jetzt vielleicht das siebte Kind
Doch jene Wolke blühte nur Minuten
Und als ich aufsah, schwand sie schon im Wind.2

MEMORY OF MARIE A.

1

That day in the blue moon of September
Still beneath a youthful tree of plums
There I held her, my pale, still beloved
Like a blessed dream within my arms.
And over in the lovely Summer sky
I saw a cloud and then I watched it long

It was so white and was extremely high
And as I gazed it vanished like a song.

2

And since that day, how many, many moons
Have softly swum beneath us and above.
The plum trees are most probably cut down
And you ask me, how does it stand with love?
I say to you: that I cannot recall
but yet, indeed, I do know what you mean.
And yet her face I would not know at all
I only know I kissed what I have seen.

3

The kiss as well, I'd have forgotten long
Were the cloud not present as we lay
That I remember and I always will
It was so white and came from far away.
The plum trees, it may be, are still in bloom
That woman has perhaps her seventh child
That cloud bloomed only for a little time
And as I looked it vanished in the wind.

This is, in fact, like Brecht's earlier Augsburg sonnets, really
a satire on love poetry. It is usual in love poetry that the
poet's meditation on the beloved leads him to contemplation of
the world around her. The pattern is here reversed. Marie A. is
really only by association with a white cloud that was passing
overhead. What the poem proclaims is only how little she meant.
The title is ironic.

This point is missed by Hannah Arendt who says:

Love, in "Memory of Marie A.," is the small pure white of a
cloud against the even purer azure blue of the Summer sky,
blooming for some instants and vanishing with the wind...To
be sure, in this world there is no eternal love or even
ordinary faithfulness. There is nothing but the intensity of
the moment; that is, passion, passion, which is even a bit
more perishable than man himself.[3]

The identification of the cloud with love is, however, never
established in the poem. The cloud and the circumstances
surrounding it are too specifically described to be taken as a
mere symbol of something else. Furthermore, Arendt's interpretation would make the love described into an exceedingly
ethereal sort, detached from any object and nearly meaningless.
For Marie A. herself, there is no feeling that the speaker is
capable of remembering. There is beauty in the poem, but the word
"passion" seems at least badly chosen. The contemplation of the
sky is too passive an activity to be described in such terms.

For an East German interpretation, we turn to Hans Kaufmann,
one of the most prominent critics in that country. Like Arendt,
he resists acknowledging the unimportance assigned to Marie A.:

The partner is explicitly removed from the current life of
the lyrical subject; somewhere she leads her own life,
perhaps in the meantime the mother of seven children--and
perhaps not.(In any case this mention establishes her human
individuality in the subject's mind.)[4]

Kaufmann refers, of course, to the final mention of her in the
last stanza. But, if anything, Brecht further depersonalizes
Marie by calling her "that woman." She is actually given about as
much "human individuality" as the plum trees, mentioned in a

similar way in the previous line. She is brought up not out of human concern but to indicate how much time has elapsed.

Kaufmann's thesis is that while the specific features of the woman have been forgotten, the encounter has been abstracted into a sort of archetypal event. The uniqueness has been lost, but the beauty has been absorbed into something universal:

> The encounter is over and unrepeatable for the lyrical subject of the poem; her (Marie's) face, however, rendered in the poetic image of a universally human and repeatable situation, is alive as a gain in humanity. The feeling is given greatness and universal validity, while Brecht simultaneously refrains from impressing raptures upon the reader, which he does not feel himself.[5]

Kaufmann is actually projecting a common East German ideal into the poem--a relationship which dispenses with human individuality yet remains warm and caring. Sexual love is reduced to human brotherhood, thus eliminating most potential conflicts between the public and private realms. What Kaufmann overlooks in his interpretation is that the central image is not the girl at all but the cloud, clearly remembered and definitely not repeatable. This is emphasized a number of times, most especially in the last two lines of the poem. It is remarkable that in the course of his interpretation Kaufmann only mentions the cloud a single time. He switches the focus back to the girl, thus depriving the poem of its novelty and its interest. If that relationship is repeatable, it is only as a vague cliche.

Both Arendt and Kaufmann fail to mention the elements of parody. One may see the influence of Heine, one of Brecht's early poetic masters. Brecht begins by building up a trite Romantic picture, only to destroy it later on. As with Heine, people have sometimes received his jokes with an attitude of utmost solemnity. There may also be some influence of Büchner, another important author for the early Brecht, who also made fun of overblown Romantic diction, employing it in incongruous ways. Elsewhere as well, Brecht often satirized classical poems and plays. This is not to say that the poem under discussion is completely devoid of sentiment. Indeed, few literary parodies are ever written without a trace of affection for their source. Parody enables the author to indulge in sentiment without the risk of appearing foolish.

In the first stanza of the poem, we find an antiquated sort of Romantic diction and imagery that is rarely used in Brecht's work. It is a literary mode that, for all its triteness, still has the power to move people, only too easily in fact. It is often hard to tell whether the mood of a poem is due to artistry or merely to the presence of such language. In the first line, there is the archaic use of "moon" for month. In the third line, he speaks of the "pale, still beloved." In the fifth, he compares her to "a holy dream." This is not the way Brecht usually writes. As one looks at the text more closely, the satiric intention becomes apparent. Only a poetic trance evoked by such Romantic diction could prevent the reader from seeing the inappropriate metaphor in the fourth line. One does not hold a dream in one's arm. In the seventh lines, the word "extremely," (ungeheuer) a somewhat more common expression, marks the first barely perceptible intrusion of prosaic reality.

If the poem appears less biting than many of Heine's lyrics, that is only because the illusion is destroyed gradually, not with a single turn of phrase. A prosaic note is struck again in the third line of the next stanza. We have the first really distinct note of sarcasm in the fourth line of the stanza, greatly muted by the melodious flow of the language but still unmistakable. Brecht seems to be chuckling softly to himself over the reader who has been taken in by the pretty words. Once more, we are reminded of Heine who would sometimes set the reader up for a punch line by throwing out a question. In the last four lines of the stanza, the author seems to be gently teasing the reader, alternately holding out and withdrawing the promise of a more elevated sentiment. The modulation of tone is very skillful.

But in the third stanza, the theme of the poem emerges unequivocally--the unimportance and insignificance of a human being in relation to nature. The cloud only is memorable and the person is trivial alongside it. It is a harsh message, made palatable and even attractive by the gentle music and the Romantic diction. It is also one of the most familiar themes in the early poems of Brecht, usually presented in a far more disturbing manner. The cosmic indifference is alternately a source of terror and relief. One is somewhat reminded of "Vom ertrunkenen Mädchen,"[6] in which the theme of the girl for-gotten--this time by God--first appears in his work.

Another poem in which Brecht adopts a relatively eloquent tone is "Die Liebenden":

DIE LIEBENDEN

Sieh jene Kraniche in großem Bogen!
Die Wolken, welche ihnen beigegeben
Zogen mit ihnen schon, als sie entflogen
Aus einem Leben in ein andres Leben.
In gleicher Höhe und mit gleicher Eile
Scheinen sie alle beide nur daneben.
Daß so der Kranich mit der Wolke teile
Den schönen Himmel, den sie kurz befliegen
Daß also keines länger hier verweile

Und keines andres sähe als das Wiegen
Des andern in dem Wind, den beide spüren
Die jetzt im Fluge beieinander liegen
So mag der Wind sie in das Nichts entführen.
Wenn sie nur nicht vergehen und sich bleiben
So lange kann sie beide nichts berühren
So lange kann man sie von jedem Ort vertreiben
Wo Regen drohen oder Schüsse schallen.
So unter Sonn und Monds wenig verschiedenen Scheiben
Fliegen sie hin, einander ganz verfallen.
Wohin, ihr?--Nirgend hin.--Von wem davon?--Von allen.
Ihr fragt, wie lange sind sie schon beisammen?
Seit kurzem.--Und wann werden sie sich trennen?--Bald.
So scheint die Liebe Liebenden ein Halt.[7]

THE LOVERS

Look up in heaven! Those cranes are flying!
The clouds which had been strewn about their path
Moved with them as the cranes were dying
To one life, entering another life
At a single height and always lying
Together, as though fate had fixed their way.
That the cranes and clouds alone divide
The lovely heaven where they briefly stay
That therefore nothing lingering should hide
The sight of one another as they sway
So may the wind sweep all into the void.
As long as they don't perish and remain
That is how long the pair cannot be touched

That is how long bullets, hail or rain
Can threaten them, if they aren't chased aside.
Though sun and moon appear to wax and wane
Onward they fly, each one the other's pride.
To where?--To nowhere--And from whom?--From all.
You ask how long they've been together now?
Not long--And when they'll be apart?--Quite soon.
So love seems to the lovers a support.

This is probably one of Brecht's most personal poems on the subject of love. It is written from the standpoint of an outsider, unable to share the sentiments in question. The lovers are distant for him. He gazes at them with a mixture of amazement, reproach, admiration and regret. They are said to run away from all. Perhaps they are irresponsible? Or perhaps the speaker really is envious of them? There is the whole vast range of emotions with which we surround the things we cannot comprehend. The poem was first published as part of the brothel scene in Mahagonny. The lines are spoken alternately by Paul and Jenny as men line up to await their turn. Framed by this carnal setting, the ideal seems both more fascinating and more absurd.

That poem is typical in respect to the ambivalence with which love is treated. The brief series entitled "Vier Liebesgedichte" may well be the only poems in the entire body of Brecht's work in which love is celebrated without sarcasm. The reticence we have spoken of may be somewhat reduced, but it has not entirely disappeared. With the sole exception of the third poem, the author speaks of his feelings in a rather abstracted way. There is no personal detail. The series, like most of Brecht's later work, does not bear the stamp of an individual personality:

VIER LIEBESLIEDER

1

Als ich nachher von dir ging
An dem großen Heute
Sah ich, als ich sehn anfing
lauter lustige Leute.

Und seit jener Abendstund,
Weißt schon, die ich meine,
Hab ich einen schönern Mund
Und geschicktere Beine.

Grüner ist, seit ich so fühl
Baum und Strauch und Wiese
Und das Wasser schöner kühl,
Wenn ich's auf mich gieße.

2

Wenn du mich lustig machst,
Dann denke ich manchmal:
Jetzt könnt ich sterben.
Dann blieb ich glücklich
Bis an mein End.

Wenn du dann alt bist
Und du an mich denkst,
Seh ich wie heut aus
Und hast ein Liebchen,
Das ist noch jung.

3

Sieben Rosen hat der Strauch,
Sechs gehör'n dem Wind.
Aber eine bleibt, daß auch
Ich noch eine find.

Sieben Male ruf ich dich,
Sechsmal bleibe fort.
Doch beim siebten Mal, versprich,
Komme auf mein Wort.

4
Die Liebste gab mir einen Zweig
Mit gelbem Laub daran.

Das Jahr, es geht zu Ende,
Die Liebe fängt erst an.[8]

FOUR LOVE POEMS

1
After, when I left you
To join the busy crowd,
When I began to see, I saw
The people, gay and loud.

And ever since that hour,
I'm sure that you know which,
My legs have grown more clever,
My lips appear more rich.

And greener, since I felt this
Are field, tree and shrub,
And pleasanter the coolness
of water in my tub.

2

When you make me laugh,
Then sometimes I think:
Now I could die.
Then I'd be happy
Until the end.

When you are old
And you think of me,
I'd look as today
And you have a beloved
Who is still young.

3

Seven roses on the bush,
Six lost in the breeze.
Only one has stayed, and waits
For me, just to please.

Seven times I call to you,
Six times stay away.
Promise me, the seventh time
Come with no delay.

4

My darling handed me a twig.
The leaves on it were brown.

The year draws to a close
And love begins to bloom.

The first of the poems is a very traditional love lyric,
rather reminiscent of Eichendorff. Though certainly quite
attractive, it does not achieve the self-assurance and naive
naturalness that we find in much of the latter's poetry. A
writer, whatever his degree of linguistic skill, tends to reveal
doubts and hesitations in subtle ways, through rhythms and
unobtrusive turns of phrase. The assurance of the second line,
something that ought to have been unnecessary, betrays a slight
lack of confidence. In terms of technique, the poem falls somewhat short of perfection. The form seems overly mechanical. This
impression is due in part to the slightly unusual feature of
having the first rime in each stanza masculine and the second
feminine. In the absence of any strong rhythmic pattern, this
creates a "sing-song" effect. The list of advantages is rattled
off a bit too automatically, making them seem less believable. In
addition to genuine sentiment, the poem probably contains a touch
of self-parody.

The second poem is by far the most personal of the series
and one of the most touching of Brecht's entire career. Unlike
the other three, it is not free of melancholy. We have the theme
of age, approaching death and nostalgia for lost youth, so
prominent in the Buckow elegies from approximately the same
period. The pathos of this poem is especially apparent when we
consider that the author was 52 when it first appeared, not so
young as the text would appear to suggest. Simply by speaking as
a younger person, Brecht was indulging in a bit of nostalgia. The
wish in the last two lines, no longer being capable of complete
fulfillment, becomes especially moving.

The third poem in the series is a sort of nursery rhyme. Nothing but its placement in the sequence actually marks it as a love poem. Because the poem is so simple, it eludes interpretation. This is part of its appeal. The lines would lose much of their lightness if any momentous import were assigned to them. Hannah Arendt called them "the one perfect product" of Brecht's last years after settling in East Berlin, implying that he had lost the ability to deal with greater themes. The language of the last poem in the series is simpler still. In its directness, it makes any attempt at learned commentary seems pedantic.

The four poems appear anything but political. Unassuming as they are, it is remarkable how much ideological significance East German critics have attached to them, the last poem especially. Because they appeared in the year after Brecht had settled in East Germany, they have been taken as indicative of a dramatic rebirth due to living in a Socialist society. Brecht is said to have turned his back on the decadence of his earlier work. Klaus Schuhmann offers the following comments:

The twig with the yellow leaves is a sign of Autumn. The change of seasons stands for the eternal cycle of nature, in which Brecht earlier had completely included the feelings of love. In 1950 the periods of nature no longer apply to love. The constancy of human feelings contrasts with the change of seasons.[9]

As an interpretation of the individual poem, this seems entirely justified. All that is questionable is the positing of such a clear break with Brecht's previous work on the basis of a single poem. Since the series occupies, as I have indicated, a rather isolated place in the body of Brecht's work, it is doubtful whether any significant biographical import can be assigned to them.

Schuhmann is comparatively restrained. Hans Kaufmann lets himself get carried away with enthusiasm for his poetic hero. Commenting on Der kaukasische Kreidekreis, he says:

> With great sensitivity, Brecht has understood that the relationship between the sexes is a delicate barometer for the general possibilities of relationships between people in the life of the society. The barometer promises good weather--the liberation from Fascism...has put the creation of a truly rational and human order on the agenda.[10]

A paragraph later, Kaufmann closes his article by commenting on the last in Brecht's series of four poems:

> Nothing speaks against an interpretation of the poem as the completely personal expression of an aging person's beginning romance. But everything speaks for also seeing, in the verses which great poets dedicate to a beloved, a reflection of their relationship to their times. The four line poem by Brecht stands as expression for a new epoch beginning in human history.[11]

He appears to give Brecht's rather modest poem and almost cosmic historical significance! There is in fact nothing in the four lines at all suggestive of historical processes. Kaufmann does not even try to explain what the beloved and the twig would, in this interpretation, represent. Here, as elsewhere, Kaufmann states his case with such fervor, such enthusiasm and such conviction that it is very hard to doubt his sincerity. Like most great illusions, this can be somewhat touching. It testifies, among other things, to the enormous emotional weight the theme of sexual love possesses, even in the political realm.

CHAPTER III

JOHANNES R. BECHER:
THE CHILD LOST IN DREAMS

In the GDR, Johannes R. Becher is generally regarded as the nation's finest poet, indeed, as one of the greatest in all of German literature. At times, his presence seems to take on almost mythic dimensions. In the West, he is remembered only for a handful of poems written early in his career. In the well-known anthology East German Poetry, Michael Hamburger does not even give Becher token representation. Born in 1891, Becher achieved moderate prominence as an Expressionist poet and coeditor with Kurt Pinthus of Die Aktion. An early convert to Marxism, he greeted the October Revolution with enthusiasm. He spent the Nazi period in Moscow, returning to become East Germany's first Minister of Culture. In his double role as a writer and public official, he was forced to draw an especially delicate balance between the demands of his artistic conscience and the requirements of orthodoxy. His position was often precarious,[1] but, after his death in 1958, he was celebrated as both a hero and a literary classic.

I regard Becher as very far from being a major poet. At the same time, I find him personally sympathetic. There is a charming naivete about his work that even political intrigues could not destroy. Much of it consists of dramatic proclamations, made as though for all eternity. Only occasionally did he depart from this declamatory style and write from experience. Becher himself was often troubled that his public prominence eclipsed his writing. While he hardly deserves comparison with his mentor Hölderlin in terms of talent, some stylistic analogies can be revealing. Both had the same high-mindedness, the same longing for immortality. Both had aspirations that are scarcely compatible with the demands of normal life, much less with the petty intrigues of a government bureaucracy.

Perhaps more than any of his contemporaries, Becher provides a record of the attitudes and illusions that were widespread at the founding of the East German state. A man of considerable passion and little subtlety, he would present everything in epic dimensions. Throughout his work, there is a constant struggle between the immortal bard and the nameless comrade. Caught between these two, the man only occasionally has opportunity to speak.

The longing for anonymity was common among the intelligentsia of the time, indeed there were few writers in the Weimar Republic whose work did not at least show traces of this. The desire was already present among the Expressionist poets, who would seek out ecstasies of self-annihilation. Artists toward the end of the Republic, those connected with the Bauhaus, for example, tended to be emotionally more restrained but continued to cultivate an impersonal quality in their work.

Like proponents of the "neue Sachlichkeit," the Communists looked for an art that would correspond to the impersonal quality of the assembly line and to a technology which inspired them with awe. Among the Communists, this desire was reinforced by the demands of party discipline. The characters in Brecht's Die Maßnahme, like those in some Expressionist dramas, do not even have names. For some writers such as Becher, the magnitude of the suffering and destruction experienced during World War II seemed to confirm their mistrust of personality. Against this background, any personal feelings whatsoever began to seem like an indulgence.

A vast poetic ambition was also not uncommon. It was an age dominated by a few individuals whose works, for good or evil, seemed to exist on a superhuman scale--Lenin, Stalin, Hitler, and others. Very extravagant claims were also made for such poets as George, Rilke and Brecht. An almost mythical greatness presented itself as a possibility, something toward which an author might strive.

Becher wrote a good deal of love poetry, most of which has little intrinsic worth. It is the pathetic record of a man who greatly longed for human warmth but was inhibited from expressing it by grandiose ideals and pressing commitments. Relationships must usually be postponed or projected into the distant future. Political terms often are used to describe private affairs. Similarly, language generally reserved for intimate relationships is carried over into politics, often creating an incongruous effect. In "Liebe ohne Ruh," for example, this latter tendency is carried to a ridiculous extreme:

LIEBE OHNE RUH

Du meine Liebe: wie verzweifelt du
Mich lieben lehrtest, und um deinen Segen
Rang ich mein Leben lang. Nur deinetwillen

Und dir zulieb nur und nur deinetwegen
Geschah mein Dasein--Liebe ohne Ruh,
Bedrängend mich bis in die tiefsten Stillen...

Du, meine Liebe: wie unsagbar ich
Dich lieben mußte! Nie war ein Begehren,
Das, mich erfüllend, dieser Liebe glich,

Und brachtest du mir auch nur Liebespein,
Ich konnte mich der Liebe nicht erwehren,
Denn dich nicht lieben wäre Nichtigsein...

Du, meine Liebe, die in jedem Lieben
Sich wiederfand und die zuoberst stand
In dem Gesetz, das mir ist eingeschrieben--

Blieb mir auch keine Qual erspart, nicht eine--
bin ich nur deine, und ich bleib ganz der deine:
Heilige Liebe du, mein Vaterland.[2]

LOVE WITHOUT REST

You my beloved, only to be blessed
By you I struggled. And how, in despair,
You taught me love and you became my quest.

I only am at all because I care
For you, and for your sake--love without rest,
The love that has pursued me everywhere...

Oh, you, my beloved, I think how immense
My love must be! I have had no desire
That, filling me, was ever so intense.

If only pain were all my love would give,
From this love, I would still have no defense,
For not to love you would be not to live...

You my beloved, of which a part
Is found in every love, the one to stand
First in that law that's written in my heart--

And if I'm not spared a single pain--
I'm only yours, and yours I will remain:
Holy beloved, you, my fatherland.

Until the last line, we assume that another person is being
addressed. If this is the case, the reference to the "fatherland"
would have to be a metaphor, a highly unusual endearment.
Czechowski actually appears to be under this impression, as he
includes the poem in his anthology of love poetry. Whether we
take this reference literally or not, it represents a confusion
of the private and public realms.

I find the poem somewhat more comprehensible if we assume
the personified country is being addressed. We then have a
nationalism that is at least coherent. But nothing in the
previous lines prepares us for the surprise ending. Had it come
at the end of a shorter poem, say two or three stanzas, the
effect might have been one of startled recognition. As it is, the
laboriously built up impression is destroyed far too abruptly.
Becher probably wished to communicate a feeling of solemnity. Our
consternation as we realize that it is not a person dissipates

any such effect. The attempt to channel personal emotions into the social arena is a disaster. Perhaps its very lack of literary quality makes this poem touching, if only as a document. The naivete with which it is conceived makes the devotion expressed seem almost convincing.

In the poem "Von Liebe und Tod," we have a similarly awkward attempt to write love poetry which dispenses with individual identity:

VON LIEBE UND TOD

Einfach wird alles:
Wir brauchen uns nichts vorzumachen.
Wir sagen, wenn etwas nicht stimmt.

Wenn wir uns
Nicht sehen vor Arbeit:
Aus meiner Arbeit siehst du mich an,
Ich sehe dich an, wenn ich arbeite.
Wir sind zusammen in der Arbeit.

Wir arbeiten für eine große gemeinsame Sache.
Wir dienen ihr mit unserem Leben.
Aus ihr kommt Liebe und Tod.

Wenn es mal so weit ist und ich es nicht mehr schaffe,
Wird ein guter Genosse für mich eintreten.

Wenn es mal so weit ist und du es nicht mehr schaffst,
Wird eine gute Genossin deinen Platz einnehmen.

Derer, die nach uns kommen, sind viele.

Starke und viele werden nach uns kommen.

Was wir halb getan haben,
Werden sie ganz machen.

Nichts wird unvollendet bleiben.

Ich freue mich, daß du in derselben Zeit lebst wie
ich. Wenn die Erde bebt, hörst auch du sie beben.
Wenn ein Gewitter aufzieht, ist es auch dein Gewitter.
Tausend Dinge nennen wir mit dem gleichen Namen.
Die Menschen, die ich kenne, sind auch dir bekannt.
Was in dich hineingesehen wird, schaut auch aus meinen
    Augen.
Deine Worte sind die meinen
In der Andersartigkeit und Vielartigkeit
Ihrer Übereinstimmung.
Wir können nicht aneinander vorübergehn.
Es gibt keine Insel, auf die wir flüchten könnten.
Wir können uns nicht verlieren.[3]

OF LOVE AND DEATH

Everything grows simple:
We don't have to pretend.
When something is wrong, we say so.

When we
Are kept apart by work:
In my work you look at me.

When I work, I look at you.
We are together in work.

We work for a great common cause,
We serve it with our lives.
From this comes life and death.

When finally I no longer can go on,
A good comrade will take my place.

When finally you no longer can go on,
A good comrade will take your place.

Those who follow us are many.
Many strong people will follow us.

What we leave half completed
They will make whole.

Nothing will remain unconsummated.

I am glad you live at the same time as I.
When the earth trembles, you also hear it tremble.
When a storm approaches, it is your storm as well.
We call thousands of things by the same name.
The people I know are also know to you.
What is seen in you also looks out through my eyes.
Your words are mine
In the differentness and the multiplicity
Of their agreement.
We cannot pass one another by.
There is no island to which we could escape.

We cannot lose each other.

The lovers are not to focus on one another but on a common goal which unites them. Only through this is their love fulfilled. Fully subordinate to this goal, their identities become interchangeable with those of other men and women who are their comrades. "Work" is presented as an almost mystical sort of sacrament. The tone, however, is so subdued it suggests resignation.

While producing such work, Becher continued to occasionally write poems from experience, through the aid of a sort of division in his personality.[4] Perhaps the constant pressure of maintaining a facade sometimes grew too much for him. He would let the mask drop, even acknowledging that much of what he said was inauthentic, as in "Du zeigst hinüber":

DU ZEIGST HINÜBER

Der Worte müd, der allzuvielen,
Weißt du: ich wehe fort im Wind,
Ich darf vor dir mit Träumen spielen,
Ich bin ein traumverspieltes Kind.

Die nie erreichte Hand erreicht mich.
Es geht sich leichter Hand in Hand.
Es geht der Weg, der schwere, leicht sich,
Weil ich dich auch als Schwester fand.

Du zeigst hinüber nach dem Hange,
Mit unserm Wein ist er bebaut.
Ich folge dir auf deinem Gange,
Du Heimatlied und Mutterlaut.

Es ist ein ungetrübtes Brennen,
Das nur mit Schweigen sich umgibt,
Und selten wag ich es zu nennen:
"Du bist für alle Zeit geliebt."5

NOW YOU POINT OVER

Enough of words, too many words,
You know: I think I'll blow away,
So let my dreams be all you heard,
I am a child lost in play.

I touch the hand I'd never touched,
The way grows easy hand in hand,
With you as sister and as friend,
The rugged path is smooth as sand.

How you point over at the slopes
Where wine we planted will be hung,
And I will follow in your steps,
You song of home, you mother tongue.

It is a bright untroubled flame
With only calm on every side,
A thing I seldom dare to name:
"Never will this love have died."

The first verse is a confession that much of his writing has been empty words, that he is lost in extravagant dreams. The reference to the mother tongue in the third stanza should not be taken literally. Though startling in its originality, the comparison of a beloved to the language does not seem strong enough to sustain an entire poem. Even in a culture like the German which endows abstract entities with exceptional vividness, it is unlikely that one love of words should take on such a directly erotic character. Mentioned in passing, however, the metaphor does suggest intimacy.

In the final verse we have a direct expression of feeling that, by his own admission, has been difficult for the author. Like much good poetry, this lyric hovers dangerously on the brink of triteness, but the ring of sincerity seems unmistakable. Even here, the somewhat surprising choice of a title indicates a wish to incorporate a political dimension, as if Becher felt slightly guilty about writing personally. The planted wine is doubtless intended to represent hopes for the future in a new society, but this is really incidental to the central theme of the poem.

CHAPTER IV

PAUL WIENS AND THE "WEATHER-VANE OF LOVE":
THE STRUGGLE FOR ARTISTIC AUTONOMY

Governments, like individuals, tend to reveal their vulnerability
in the things that provoke them to indignation. Seldom has an
essentially unpolitical book provoked such an intense reaction as
did Nachrichten aus der dritten Welt by Paul Wiens. In a 1958
special edition of Weimarer Beiträge, a highly regarded East
German journal that is usually restricted to scholarly discussion
of established authors, an article by Dieter Schiller on emerging
writers was printed. Kuba was praised for championing the cause
of Socialism in his propagandistic poems. Wiens was singled out
as the subject of a furious attack. The gist of it was that Wiens
had neglected the class-struggle and the Socialistic cause, giving himself over to bourgeois individualism. There are a number
of reasons to think that Schiller was not merely expressing an
individual opinion but an official viewpoint. The article was no
doubt intended to inform writers of what was desirable and what
might not be tolerated, using Kuba and Wiens respectively as
examples. For one thing, such current subject matter was unusual
for this particular publication, indicating that the article had

a purpose and importance that went a little beyond the ordinary. There is also the fact that Schiller's criticism ignored aesthetic considerations entirely, concentrating on the political messages that were supposedly implicit in the poems. It is the statement of a party bureaucrat whose interests are not of an artistic nature and who probably could not conceive of poetry serving any purpose other than the crudest propaganda. Perhaps part of the reason for Schiller's bitterness was that Wiens appeared to be an apostate. Wiens' first book, <u>Beredte</u> <u>Welt</u> had been given the Goethe prize. It closed with a rather long poem entitled "Gruß an Stalin,"[1] certainly one of the more extravagant hymns of praise that Stalin had ever received.

Wiens' second collection, the one that provoked Schiller's attack, contained a section entitled "Aus den neuen Harfenliedern des Oswald von Wolkenstein," in which the persona of Oswald, a late medieval poet, is adopted. This assumed identity was a device to shield Wiens from criticism by limiting his own responsibility. He indicates this himself in the following lines from his poetic introduction.:

> Der Wolkensteiner mag mir
> die Maskerade übelnehmen,
> Sie bitte nicht!
> Im Kostüm
> läßt sich
> --das beweisen
> auch unsere Feste--
> oft freier lieben
> und mit Ernst schabernacken.[2]

The man from Wolkenstein
may take my masquerade badly,
please don't you!
In a costume
one can
--that is also proved
by our celebrations--
often love more freely
and be jokingly earnest.

But Schiller was not going to let him get away with this! Instead of excusing Wiens, Schiller went on to blame him for Oswald's faults. Rather than take the persona as a gay masquerade, Schiller asserted that Oswald had become the "model for Wiens' life philosophy,"[3] replacing the patriarchs of Socialist literature. The late medieval poet represents, in Schiller's view, the individual who stands apart from society.

Wiens had certainly not intended the identification with Oswald to be so absolute. It was a joke, not entirely unlike the fantastic tales with which Oswald himself would embellish his travelogues. What attracted Wiens to Oswald was not so much the latter's "individualism" or any such general quality. If such had been the case, there would have been a great number of more prominent poets whose work could have served at least as well. Oswald was picked for his reputation as "the last of the minnesingers."

The poem from the collection which probably provoked the greatest anger was "Minnewetterhahn":

MINNEWETTERHAHN

Ist denn die Minne, frag ich, matt geworden,

der leise, tolle, lebenslange Klang?
Tief in das Eis drang ich im hohen Norden
mit Boris, und ich fand--nichts von Belang.
Und er, der einst die grünen Augen suchte,
grub Tunnels, legte Schienen und vergaß,
bald kälter als der Pol, den er verfluchte,
die grünen Augen und das grüne Gras.

Auch Farrady, der wilde Blumen jagt,
ein heimatloser Mensch, Irrlicht im Süden,
hat mich nach Mitternacht am Fluß gefragt:
--Was sind die Träume wert, wenn sie ermüden?
Ich hatte siebzehn, die ich ganz besaß.
Und alle waren treu, und keine lastet
dem leeren Pulse mehr, der sinnlos hastet,
Die Orchideen duften, doch nach Aas.--

Bei uns zulande, an der Weltenscheide,
traf ich Franz Lebrecht, ein gerades Kreuz,
der sich entschied, und steht zu seinem Eide
bei Staat und Frau, treu steht er und bereut's.
Und voller Vorsicht, wenn das Lenzweh kommt,
erbebt sein Herz und fürchtet die Gebresten
und schlägt das Fieber nieder, das nicht frommt.
So steht es mit der Liebe hier im Westen.

Nur der Student im Teehaus "Grüne Schlange"
sann höflich nach, erhob sich und gestand:
--Wir kämpften, hungerten, marschierten lange.
Ich weiß nicht, was du fragst. Ich bin ein Sand,
ein Korn, das ruht und rieselt unter vielen.
Heut bin ich satt und habe freie Zeit.

Ich kenne Minne nicht noch Mattigkeit,
doch Mädchenaugen wohl, die mir gefielen...

Komm, fremder Dichter, laß uns Ping-Pong spielen![4]

THE WEATHER-VANE OF LOVE

Has courtly love, I ask you, now grown weak,
the crazy, quiet, constant, life-long ring?
Covered with ice, I climbed a Northern peak
with Boris and I found--hardly a thing.
And he who used to search for the green eyes
forgot while digging tunnels, moving goods,
cold as the very Pole he despised,
the green of eyes, the green and brown of woods.

And Farrady who chased the wild rose,
a will-o'-wisp that wanders in the South,
asked me past midnight where the water flows:
If they must fade, what can the dreams be worth?
I had eighteen, and I possessed the lot
and all of them were true, but none could stay
the empty pulse that blindly beats away.
In orchids I can smell--nothing but rot.

And here at home, we are touching both.
I met Franz Lebrecht, like an upright cross,
who gave his word and would not break his oath
to state and wife, but only at a loss,
for spring would make him circumspect and sad.

His heart would start to beat against the breast.
He'd beat the fever down and call it bad,
and this is how we know love in the West.

A student in the tea-house "Serpent-Green"
politely thought, then rose and told me plain:
Long marches, battles, hunger I have seen.
I don't know what you mean. I am a grain,
a corn that, with the others, moves along.
Now I have eaten and have time to spare.
I don't know love, but am set free of care,
and girl's eyes that might inspire song...?

Come, foreign poet, let us play ping-pong!

The poet begins his search for courtly love in the Soviet Union.
Against a background of extravagant claims that were constantly
being made for Soviet accomplishments, the casual assertion that
the author had found nothing of importance may have seemed more
damning than any direct attack. There are a number of veiled
criticisms of Soviet society, things that Schiller did not try to
rebut or even mention, no doubt because this would have involved
making them explicit. Wiens seems to regard the difficulty of
love as symptomatic of other fundamental difficulties. This is
suggested by the poem's title. Sexual love is to be taken as a
"weather-vane," pointing the general direction in which society
is moving. Wiens attacks the incessant emphasis on work that was,
and to an extent still is, a constant feature of Soviet propaganda. Even at this, the criticism does not seem quite strong
enough to explain the furious reply which it provoked. The fact
that the poem is set on the Pole rather than in Russia proper
might suggest a reference to the Stalinist labor camps. It

is true that, had Wiens known of these, a far less playful response would have been indicated. What would then have to be explained is not Wiens' rebellion but his general loyalty to the East German state. It is even conceivable that the lines may reflect an unconscious awareness of something that Wiens would not acknowledge to himself. If poetry is, as most psychologists and lyricists believe, closely linked with the unconscious, poetry should be able to reveal not only unsuspected emotion but also knowledge. Schiller perhaps had this possibility in mind when he wrote:

In this poem is...contained the entire arsenal of revisionist distortions, not open, direct, but hidden, in the orientation, perhaps not even fully conscious.[5]

The article is full of such general statements which are never very precisely explained but could be read as a warning to the initiate.

The second stanza of Wiens' poem is fully in accord with the party line. The decadence of Capitalist society is seen as precluding love. Instead, there is only a dreary succession of sexual relationships. But in the third stanza, Wiens takes Germany to task for making love impossible through an overly rigid morality. Schiller comments:

...he (Wiens) sticks to an individualistic irony and rejects the norms of Social ethics and morality.[6]

This fails to recognize that Wiens' critique encompasses both the Socialist and Capitalist parts of Germany. We must remember that the poems were written some time before the erection of the Berlin Wall. Many people still looked forward to an eventual union between the Allied and Soviet sectors, but the authorities in East Germany wished to establish a distinct national identity. The idea that all of Germany could be encompassed in a single critique was resented.

It seems peculiar, though perhaps not uncharacteristic, that what is rejected should be referred to by Schiller as "the norm of Socialist ethics and morality." The stanza actually describes a familiar stereotype of the German bourgeoisie. There is not a single element here that is unique to Socialism.

The only country in which the speaker in Wiens' poem finds any hope at all is China. Schiller's reaction is about what might have been expected:

The way out is finally seen in tolerance, as it is supposedly practiced in China and not in the Soviet Union--a thesis that is not far removed from the view that China is the leading country of the Socialist camp, a dangerous anti-Soviet view that has long prevailed among some intellectuals, because they did not know or understand the complicated class-struggle in the People's Republic of China.7

The ending of the poem is actually much more ambiguous than this. The final line is a rather playful anticlimax that could indicate either curiosity or a real lack of interest. One might just as well see the diversion offered at the end as a final frustration of the speaker's quest.

Whatever implications Wiens may have actually intended, the meaning that Schiller sees in these lines is revealing. Saying that love is more possible in China than in the Soviet Union is viewed as practically the equivalent of making China the rightful leader of the Socialist movement. Part of the reason for seeing such an implication is certainly a nervous sensitivity to any possible attack on Soviet authority. It is doubtless also the great emotional weight carried by sexual love. Such a criticism, whatever its pragmatic or ideological base, would, on a purely emotional level, constitute a very strong condemnation of the Soviet Union. The state would lose our sympathy like the feuding aristocrats in Romeo and Juliet. Wiens had obviously touched upon a nerve. Another reason why Wiens' book appeared threatening is the format in which it was presented. It was part of a series published by Verlag Volk und Welt, edited by Marianne Dreifuß and Wiens himself, with the explicit purpose of encouraging contact with the readers. On the back cover of Wiens' book, the two editors have placed the following statement:

> This series of modern poetry is supposed to promote living contact between poet and reader. Please write to us...

Next to this is a postcard already addressed to the publisher. On both the cover and the title page, the appeal for an answer is repeated. Wiens had, it would seem, not intended for the ideas embodied in his work to be ignored, but the authorities felt threatened by precisely this sort of contact.

The attack by Schiller did not end Wiens' career, although he was deprived of his position as editor within a year.[8] Wiens' completed Die neuen Harfenlieder von Oswald von Wolkenstein was published in 1966, eight years after Nachrichten aus der Dritten Welt. In the course of years, Wiens' was gradually rehabilitated. In an essay first published 1965 in Neutralität, Rainer Kirsch complained publicly that the collected work of Wiens had not appeared because of his justified refusal to remove a poem, rejected "for unclear reasons."[9] Wiens' collected works was actually published in 1968 under the title Dienstgeheimnis:

Ein Nächtebuch. The Oswald poems were not included. Wiens did not, however, simply let them be forgotten. In a brief preface, he says:

> The inclination to the loose and light, the slant toward the bitter-biting, on which I am only too fond of tobogganing, I will open again, dear legion of readers, for your use at the first good opportunity, next. For this reason, you will not find here the texts that have not yet been set to music but would be suited to it, all solo-, choir-, dance-, film-, cabaret-, march-, children's-, battle-, youth-, sport-, festival-, record- and song-book melodies. Therefore, the new "Songs for Harp of Oswald von Wolkenstein" can, for the time being, circulate uncollected, long and large is life, my art short and small, they will make their way and either perish or survive...10

Like many publications in East Germany, this one is surrounded by a bit of mystery. In the passage which I have just quoted and in the introductions to individual sections of his book, Wiens presents a whimsical but obscure defense of his poetics. The presence of censorship often causes authors to "write in code," employing references that are likely to escape the authorities but will be clear to a certain select public. The obscurity and some what artificial tone, as well as Wiens' avowed use of humor to convey a serious message, suggest the presence of such references here.

In 1969 Weimarer Beiträge paid Wiens, by then a well-established writer, the compliment of devoting much of an issue to his work. Reinhard Weisbach recapitulated Schiller's criticism, concluding that the reproach of individualism was somewhat justified. Weisbach then proceeded with a reasonably sensitive analysis of Wiens' poetry, finding considerable value in it.[11] Weisbach appears as a sort of mediator, smoothing the way between the previous rejection of Wiens' poetry and the new acceptance of it. One might indeed wonder how Schiller could be taken seriously enough to be granted such a thoughtful rebuttal, but this is a paradox of GDR literature. There is a sense of common endeavor which seems to encompass both liberals and Stalinists, both esthetes and propagandists.

In the somewhat more liberal atmosphere of 1976, Wiens finally republished "Minnewetterhahn" and the other Oswald poems in an extensive collection entitled Vier Linien aus meiner Hand. The only texts missing from this book were the early propagandistic poems with which he had begun his career. His introduction to the Oswald poems may be taken as a final reply to Schiller:

> In 1955 I spoke with Oswald about the congress of writers then in progress. In spite of my requests, he was not to be moved from his refusal to render his opinion about poetry in any form but life and song. But I will nevertheless give an extract from our conversation, point by point. First, the writer cannot comprehend his time abstractly, he can only comprehend it as a writer..." Secondly, Os quoted a Russian by the name of Lenin who is supposed to have said in his last essay "Rather less but better": "in questions of culture there is nothing more damaging than haste and superficiality. That ought to be written behind the ears of many of your young literati and Communists..."[12]

If some party official is skeptical about Oswald's sudden conversion to orthodoxy, I cannot greatly blame him.

It is extremely likely that the attack by Schiller actually helped Wiens' career in the long run by drawing attention to his work. People often take any strong reactions to a work of art as evidence of aesthetic value. "Minnewetterhahn" is, however, a rather undistinguished poem that, apart from its political implications, would hardly have merited such attention. The portraits in it are all somewhat stereotyped. The form is overly mechanical. There is little rhythmic variation. Though it was rather daring to express them in such a context, the ideas in the poem are far from original.

Of the more prominent East German poets, the great majority have run into some political trouble at one point or another during their careers. This is not necessarily disastrous, as our example illustrates. The pattern is actually similar to what we often find in the non-Communist world, where many young writers begin by attacking an establishment they will later join. Wiens is now numbered among the foremost poets of his native land. A skillful though not greatly inspired writer, he may well be overheated. Along with Christa Wolf, Wiens came to be considered a spokesperson for those writers who accept their country's foreign policy and ideology but insist on greater artistic autonomy. His status as a liberal activist was, however, somewhat tarnished in 1976 when he became one of the few writers of any prominence to support unequivocally the expulsion of dissident poet Wolf Biermann. By his death in 1982, Wiens was often considered the most urbane and sophisticated defender of the status quo.

CHAPTER V

GEORG MAURER'S "FIGURES OF LOVE":
ESCAPE INTO THE MARXIST IDYLL

Georg Maurer is one East German poet whose work seem to stand
precisely at the intersection of Marxism and Christianity. Born
1907 into a Lutheran home in "Siebenbürgen" or Transylvania, he
moved to Berlin as a young man to study Art History and began an
intellectual development which is representative for several
modern thinkers and poets. The Christian perspective of his
earliest work soon gave way, under the influence of Rilke, to a
Romantic Humanism pervaded by a sense of "Weltschmerz." This in
turn was replaced, during Soviet occupation, by Marxism. What is
remarkable is how undramatically these changes have taken place.
Only by means of his theoretical statements can they even be
clearly distinguished. The Romanticism of Maurer is so close to
both Marxism and Christianity that the change from one to another
appears only as a slight shift in orientation. Until his death in
1971, Maurer retained an affection for Christianity. He seems to
have had an extremely sensitive and pious nature of the sort that
craves an orthodoxy, something to which the individual may
subordinate himself. But the nature of this orthodoxy seems,

paradoxically, rather arbitrary. Like Christianity, Marxism has often shown the flexibility to accommodate many different interpretations.

The fact that Maurer did not learn literary German until the age of nine may explain the formality of his language. Unusually free of any conversational idioms, it has a sort of scholarly majesty. His background as an art-critic could be responsible for the static, picture-like quality of his poems. He never communicates a sense of continuous motion. At most there is a succession of isolated moments, each of them fixed in time. The absence of irony and ambiguity set Maurer apart from most twentieth century writing. Drawing on traditions foreign to most of his countrymen and possessed of an original vision, he was able to create a unique body of work.

In East Germany itself, Maurer is among the most greatly admired poets. His disciples include such distinguished lyricists as Czechowski, Mickel and Rainer Kirsch. He is sometimes even accorded the veneration that Germans have traditionally bestowed on poets such as Goethe, Schiller, Hölderlin but has been granted to no West German poet since the end of World War II. At the same time, Maurer has received remarkably little attention in the West.

The reason is, I believe, cultural rather than political. Maurer, more than any other important poet since 1945, belongs to an essentially Romantic tradition in which the poet assumes a prophetic role. It is his task to animate an otherwise prosaic world. Such an ambitious mission was claimed, at least implicitly by a long line of German poets such as Hölderlin, George, Trakl and Rilke, but the tradition appears to have died in West Germany today. There is an innocence in Maurer's work that is very difficult to maintain now in the West, an almost childlike trust in his traditions and in his calling. The elevated style of

Maurer's verse has only found a receptive audience in the GDR where the poetic vocation continues to inspire a sort of awe. Even the way in which writers are harassed and feared suggests respect for their power. The prophetic gesture has no doubt been sanctioned by the example of Marx himself, whose style often invites comparison with figures from the Old Testament.

Maurer's poetry finds a philosophical equivalent in the writing of Ernst Bloch. The vast tomes of this thinker center around a single theme--the longing for the absolute. In his terminology, this is called "hope" (Hoffnung), although he would not allow for the uncertainty which this word generally presupposes. He finds hope manifest in daydreams, in sexual love, in art and in all aspects of human culture. Bloch views these things as an anticipation of an eventual transfiguration of all reality, identified with the Marxist utopia.

Such longing is the trademark of Romanticism. The Marxists have from the beginning, tended to be no less uncompromising in their aspirations than the Romantics. The important difference is that Marx and his immediate followers expressed comparatively little doubt that their aspirations were attainable. Most of the Romantics, on the other hand, have recognized the enormous distance of their ideals from the world they knew, and despaired of ever closing it. Novalis and Eichendorff are possibly exceptions. As a result, the Romantics were inclined toward melancholy. For Bloch, the longing for perfection carried its own promise of fulfillment. The Marxian insistence on an ultimate identity of mind and matter would insure that dreams must come true. The only progressive or realistic attitude was, he believed, one of extreme optimism. This also became his moral imperative.

The philosophy of Bloch touched on Existentialism. The existence of imperfection showed, he believed, that the world is still in the process of creation. It exists in relation to the void, the nothingness which is identified with everything negative. Hope is said to carry with it a despair no less absolute than the promise it contains. Nevertheless, there is no doubt that this nothingness will be overcome.

Bloch also opened the way for a synthesis of Marxism and Christianity. The time was, in any case, growing ripe for this. Marxism had embarked on a course of development very similar to that of early Christianity. Like the early Christians, the Marxists have had to deal with a constant postponement of the millennium. As the Marxist utopia is pushed into the ever more indefinite future, the difference between the two systems of belief is gradually diminished. Marxists increasingly regard Communism as an abstract ideal by which to orient oneself, rather than a concrete reality. From this perspective, it is primarily the position of Christ which distinguishes Christianity from Marxism. In the work of Bloch, even this difference starts to disappear. Christ, he believed, represented a significant advance in the movement toward a historical utopia. By his very existence, Christ affirmed the Marxist belief in mankind's essential goodness, thereby anticipating the ideal world that is still to come.

During the war, Bloch emigrated to the United States. Shortly after the Nazi defeat, he moved to East Berlin, where he collected an intellectual following and became a center of controversy. The vast sweep of his ideas added excitement to his works. More conventional Marxists pointed out that he ignored the economic side of Marxism entirely. Despite the suspicion with which he was regarded, the orthodoxy of his political views made him for a time, acceptable to the authorities. The flights of poetic imagination in his work were interspersed with tributes to Marx and Lenin. In the crackdown which followed the abortive Hungarian Revolution, political orthodoxy was no longer enough to protect Bloch. Lecturing in the West when the Berlin Wall was erected in 1961, he decided not to return home.

Bloch left East Germany with a cultural legacy that continued after he was repudiated. The ideas of the philosopher and even many of his stylistic characteristics are to be found in the work of Maurer. Take, for example, the following poem:

DER PFIRSICH

Meine Sinne wenden sich der Welt zu.
Taub wollten sie sein. Sind wieder fröhlich,
neugierig wie ein Kind, das in der Hand
der Erwachsenen etwas erwartet voll
schönster Unbestimmtheit. Auf meinem Tisch
find ich einen Pfirsich: Unendlichkeit
in goldener Kugel...![1]

THE PEACH

My senses open to the world.
They wished to be deaf, are glad again,
curious like a child that expects
something in the grow-up's hand, full
of glorious uncertainty. On my table
I find a peach: Eternity
in a golden ball...!

This is typical for the way in which Bloch as well would find longing for the absolute in the most unexpected places, from works of art to the homier details of everyday life. There is also the idea that optimism follows naturally when one is receptive to the sensuous world, a fundamental tenet of Bloch's philosophy.

It is hard to tell how much of the similarity to Bloch is due to a direct influence. This may have been considerable. From 1955 on, Maurer taught at the Johannes R. Becher Institute in Leipzig, an institution at which Bloch was also employed. If Maurer never proclaimed himself Bloch's disciple, this might be explained by the latter's uncertain reputation. Such a declaration would have threatened Maurer's career. Maurer does cite Bloch frequently in a report on the fourth Congress of German Authors,[2] indicating at least some familiarity with his work. We should remember that the Eat German literary community is far more circumscribed than that of the United States, Britain or even the Federal Republic. It tends to be dominated by a relatively small number of authors, making confrontation with the ideas of an important figure like Bloch difficult to avoid. Nevertheless, it is also possible that the similarity between Maurer and Bloch may be due primarily to the intellectual climate of their times. Certain ideas could have simply found their articulation almost simultaneously in the work of these two writers.

Maurer's essays reveal the same combination of unfettered imagination and strict orthodoxy that we find in Bloch. His considerable originality is shown by the manner in which he interprets the patriarchs of Communism, never in a questioning of them. As with Bloch and so many others in the GDR, it is impossible to know how much Maurer may have concealed his true opinions on pragmatic grounds. I am inclined to believe that his orthodoxy was quite sincere. He needed the security of a fixed set of beliefs to indulge in such free play of the imagination.

Salvation through absolute love is a literary theme that is closely associated with the Romantic tradition. This identification has even determined the meaning of the word "Romantic" in the popular mind. It is even stronger if we use the conception of Romanticism employed by English-speaking critics, who, in contrast to the Germans, include Goethe, Schiller and Hölderlin among the representatives of that movement. The theme has largely disappeared from modern poetry in the Western world, but tends to be more cultivated in the East. Few poets have pursued it more persistently than Maurer. At the same time, his celebrations of love have an abstracted quality which sets them apart from traditional love lyrics. The concept of love is continuously changed, refined and reexamined in his work. It is introduced in several contexts and overlaid with different associations, acquiring eventually a meaning far beyond the usual. Rather than simply a feeling, love is seen as an active power that creates reality and contains the promise of a better world. Dieter Schlenstedt has pointed out that, for Maurer, the opposite of love is not hate but "Angst,"[3] a term denoting something between fear and anguish, not quite translatable with "anxiety." Maurer identifies this with "nothingness" or "the void" (das Nichts). By this time, we may recognize in "love," as Maurer uses the word, a very close equivalent to Bloch's concept of hope. The latter also exists in relationship to the void, the source of despair. Both writers derive a demand for optimism from their central concepts. Finally, they both share a similar closeness to Christianity, absorbed into the Marxist framework. The cosmology in Maurer's poetry is, in fact, hardly more than the philosophy of Bloch restated using a somewhat different terminology.

Schlenstedt recognizes all of the features that I have spoken of in his rather detailed elucidation Maurer's work. He does not, however, mention Bloch at all. The similarity between Bloch and Maurer is so striking that it seems surprising Schlenstedt should have overlooked it entirely. It is at least possible that Schlenstedt may have been aware of this, but refrained from mentioning it as a pragmatic accommodation. Any close association with the philosophy of Bloch would have largely discredited Maurer, and perhaps Schlenstedt as well, in the eyes of the GDR cultural authorities. Like Lukacs, Bloch was to have many of his ideas developed by others who chose not to acknowledge their source.

"Gestalten der Liebe" (Figures of Love) is a series of poems by Maurer, examining love in various manifestations. In the final four lines of the first poem, love is presented as a humanizing force:

Wenn wir den Mund mit dem Mund wie eine Beute halten,
die Zahnreihe sanft in die Lippe senken
und die Hände uns drücken bis zur Grenze von Süße und
    Schmerz,
Geliebte, empfinde da, wie die Liebe
durch die Welt geht
und die Linien des Menschlichen einzeichnet,
die Bojen in die Strömung des Alls senkt,
daß wir passieren auf heiterer Flotte das Weltmeer--
denn nicht verläßlich ist die Schale der Erde
und das Wasser darin und das Wetter, das über ihm
    dampft--
zwar wir können seine Launen voraussehn...
Du aber fragst mich, und ich frage dich immer:
Was kann ich dir Liebes tun, darf

ich mich freun an dir?--Ach, so fragen nicht
die Elemente und die Stierhäuptigen unter den Menschen,
denn die rasen und keuchen, und ihr Friede ist nur
ihr Erschöpftsein oder der Tod unterm Fallbeil der
  Völker.
Wir aber nennen Liebe lebendigen Frieden,
der erfinderisch macht und die Kräfte so führt,
daß sie einrichten das Zimmer mit freundlichen Vorhängen
und die Blumen stellen in die Schale mit frischem Wasser.

When we hold mouth to mouth as if it were a prey, sink
the row of teeth softly into the lip
and press our hands to the limits of sweetness and pain,
beloved, consider then how love
goes through the world
and marks off bounds of the human realm,
sinks the buoy in the current of space,
that our cheerful fleet may navigate the sea--
for the crust of earth is not to be trusted,
nor the water in it, nor the weather fuming above it--
true, we can guess what its moods will be . . .
But you ask me, and I ask you ever again:
What can I do for you out of love, may
I be happy with you?--Ah, that is not asked
by the elements or by bull-headed men,
for they pant and gasp, and only find peace
in exhaustion or death under the executioner's blade.
But we call love that active peace
that calls to creation and so guides our hands
that they furnish the room with attractive curtains

and place flowers in a vase with fresh water.4

To test the closeness to Bloch's philosophy, the reader may choose to read this--or, for that matter, any poem in the series--substituting the word "hope" for "love." He will find that there is very little loss in coherence and that the meaning is hardly changed.

A Blochian sort of optimism finds especially strong expression in the last nine lines of the third poem:

so streiften meine Lippen deine Wange,
bis mein Mund mit deinem sich traf:
die Geburt der Bewegung!
und ist nicht jedem ein Entgegen
bestimmt, der Sehnsucht die Heilung,
meinem Durst dein Trank, meinem Gang dein Warten?
Dieses vertrauliche Wissen der Menschheit von der
    Bewegung,
diese Bewegung um die Vertraulichkeit der Welt,
diese Begegnung unserer innigsten Wünsche!

your cheek was brushed by my lips,
till my mouth had met yours:
the beginning of motion!
And is not a response for all
prepared, for longing, salvation;
my thirst, your drink;
my stride, your waiting?
This is mankind's intimate knowledge of motion,
this motion about the trust of the world,

this meeting of our innermost wishes.[5]

It is difficult or impossible to trace any linear development in Maurer's series. Even the individual poems are only very loosely organized. This may reflect the influence of Bloch in the aesthetic as well as in the intellectual realm. The latter's major work entitled Das Prinzip Hoffnung is an extensive survey of all hope's manifestations. These are hardly more sequential than when we encounter them in real life. It is a kind of philosophy that verges very close on being poetry. One does not find arguments that can be isolated and criticized. This quality of Bloch's work is emphasized by both critics and admirers. In his history of Marxism, Leszek Kolakowski calls Bloch "a preacher of intellectual irresponsibility," adding that "on the rare occasion when he puts forth an argument, it usually reveals his intellectual helplessness."[6] But precisely the quality that Kolakowski condemns constitute the attraction of Bloch's philosophy for the writer Martin Walser, according to whom Bloch "developed a method with which every occurrence is again deprived of its crude positivistic qualities."[7] Das Prinzip Hoffnung tries to convince largely through its artistic appeal. The lack of a strict sequence makes reading Bloch into an adventure. On can hardly guess what will come next. This quality is also to be found in Maurer. The manifestations of love are not presented in any systematic order. It is shown in the heavens and in ordinary life, in relation to couples, works of art, animals and children.

The technique used by both writers is the opposite of what we find in most traditional philosophy. Most philosophers try to give a concept greater precision by progressively limiting the contexts in which it may be used. Both Bloch and Maurer gradually expand their central concepts, using them in every possible connection. The meaning of the concept becomes increasingly rich but inexact. Maurer pays homage to love by making it the starting point of his ascent, but one may question whether this is truly his theme. He seems to avoid personal experience by moving to ever greater levels of abstraction.

Maurer is in ways a puzzling poet. It seems very surprising that a man who lived through Nazi Germany, the fall of Berlin and the reign of Stalin could write poems that are consistently so delicate and sensitive. The sweetness and optimism of his work must be regarded somewhat skeptically. If the traumatic times that Maurer lived through are reflected in his poetry, it is through the absence of distinctly personal experience. We may guess that a threatening environment forced him to turn inward, giving his poems an abstracted character. The imagery, beautiful though it is, tends to be drawn from books. The exotic and places add considerable color to his work but also invite the charge of escapism. There are few images drawn from the modern or industrial world. These tend to be idealized. The poems contain hardly any references to specific people, places or events that Maurer was acquainted with. This abstracted character tends to be prized in the Socialist world, which de-emphasizes purely individual experience, but I believe that it has limited Maurer's scope. Rather than transcending individuality, he merely ignores it. One aspect of sexual love is an intense awareness of personal uniqueness. It is especially here that people are not interchangeable. Maurer fails to communicate this. There is none of the sort of detail which would give people or events the impression of individuality. Like most of the finest poets, Maurer is able to give human experience a cosmic dimension. Unfortunately, in the process of doing this, he deprives this experience of its individual character.

Another thing that makes Maurer's optimism less convincing in "Gestalten der Liebe" is his probably unconscious habit of switching to the third person whenever negative sentiments are expressed, suggesting that he entertained these but would not confess to them. One unusual feature of these poems is that they are mostly written in the first person plural, not in the more usual "Lyrical I." The author usually seems to be speaking for himself and a beloved, sometimes for all men and women. The identity of the voice is ambiguous, perhaps to indicate the fluid boundaries of the self. But whenever a pessimistic note is struck, as in the sixth and seventh poems, the poet attributes these sentiments to another person. The "we" is replaced by "they" or "you." At most, the speaker suffers vicariously. All negative emotions are projected outward.

The criticism most often made of Romantic poets is that their work is too ethereal. What Maurer has done is to continue the Romantic tradition while eliminating the one major characteristic which kept them rooted in this world--their pessimism. He presents an extremely Romantic vision, but, unlike most of the Romantics, he does not seem to recognize the gap between this and reality. Although his series of poems attempts to include all manifestations of love, the more earthy and prosaic aspects are missing. Such things as sex, jealousy and the little strains on a relationship that come in the course of everyday life have no place in this conception. The vision put forth by Maurer is beautiful and noble. The question is whether people can live by it. Such poems, like the hymns of Hölderlin, tend to leave us very unsatisfied with the world as it is. They can inspire us, but the discontent is not always productive. It can also lead to depression. Hölderlin was very aware of this problem and sought desperately to overcome it, giving his work a tragic dimension. Maurer often seems to have lost sight of the distinction between experience and imagination. He describes a world in which most things are beautiful and all are really purposeful and good.

Maurer is perhaps the most gifted poet ever to have resided in East Germany. With his intellect, consummate technical skill and delicate sensibility, he might easily have become the great poet that his countrymen sometimes take him for. What is lacking is only the spiritual courage which the finest poetry requires.

CHAPTER VI

HEINZ KAHLAU'S DU:
THE DENIAL OF INDIVIDUALITY

Since the founding of the East German state, attempts have
constantly been made to bring children of the working class into
the ranks of successful authors. Among the most prominent of
these has been Heinz Kahlau. At first an unskilled laborer, he
became a heavy equipment operator. In 1953, at the age of 22, he
began study under Brecht. He is often compared with his master,
both with respect to content and to style. He shares the didactic
concern and the extreme linguistic simplicity that we find in the
later work of Brecht, but has little of the latter's inven-
tiveness. As a poet, Kahlau does not seem to have changed or
developed much in the course of his career. On the other hand,
Kahlau does seem to have some of the simple humanity which Brecht
wished so badly to achieve but, in my opinion, never could. In
contrast to the extreme complexity and elusiveness of Brecht's
personality, Kahlau seems comparatively without artifice. His
poems are well-crafted and unprecedented. Above all, Kahlau seems
to lack Brecht's bitterness. His poems employ only the gentler
sorts of irony, never angry sarcasm.

In a collection of his love poetry entitled Du, Kahlau has produced far more than a number of isolated lyrics. Presenting sexual love in several everyday contexts, Kahlau makes a fairly systematic attempt to address the problem that has troubled nearly all who have written love poetry in East Germany: How can an experience which sets two people apart from the rest avoid the reproach of being antisocial? The ambivalent nature of sexual love has created a good deal of embarrassment and uncertainty with in the Socialist world. It is a social bond that cannot easily be dispensed with, but it can distract people from the public realm. Kahlau is trying to present an ideal in which this tension is overcome.

In a sense these are not love poems at all but parodies of them. This would place the poems in a tradition of profane poetry that goes back at least to the early Italian Renaissance and continues as a counterweight to the exalted traditions of courtly love. In Germany, leading figures in this tradition have been Neidhart von Reuenthal and, to a great extent, Heinrich Heine. It includes most of Brecht's love poetry, the Augsburg sonnets for example. These poets would make fun of Romantic spirituality by emphasizing the coarser aspects of sexuality, something that is completely absent from Kahlau's collection. Instead of using sensuality as a counter to Romantic visions, Kahlau uses the prosaic demands of everyday life. In an interview with Mathilde Dau, Kahlau has stated that his love poems are the product of thoughts rather that feelings, an approach he claims to have learned from Brecht.[1]

Despite the fact that these poems are written as an answer to traditional love lyrics, the restrained style makes one hesitate to place them in the tradition that I have mentioned. The parody is gentle, at times almost affectionate. It would probably be more accurate to say that Kahlau is trying to synthesize the sacred and the profane traditions.

Already in the dedication (to Irene G.), Kahlau challenges
traditional expectations from a book of love poems:

Nicht eine Zeile
schreib ich nur dir
zum Gefallen.
Denn meine Verse
gehören mir
oder allen.[2]

I will not write
a single line
simply to please you.
For my verses
belong to me
or to all.

This is the exact opposite of what a poet, under such circumstances, has been expected to say. Kahlau's point is that even
in love poems, too much exclusive emphasis ought not to be placed
on the other person.

The first poem in the volume is entitled "Ich liebe dich"
and ends with a criticism of a more Romantic conception:

Ich liebe dich
heißt immer:
Ich will dich
für etwas haben,
das mir Glück verspricht.
Manchmal entsteht daraus:
Wir lieben uns.
Erst dieser Satz

hat wirkliches Gewicht.3

I love you
always means:
I want you
for something
that will make me happy.
Sometimes this leads to:
We love each other.
Only this sentence
has real importance.

Kahlau deliberately uses such highly impersonal language as a sort of "alienation effect." There is, he suggests, something at least potentially selfish about love. In the case of unrequited love, it is self-centered to dwell on one's own feelings. Only when love is mutual does it begin to lose this narcissistic character.

Kahlau's primary departure from traditional love lyrics lies in his continual use of understatement. Nevertheless, he sometimes recognizes love as an enormous power, as in the closing of "Die Liebe":

Freilich--
uns selber zu ändern,
sind Kräfte vonnöten,
mit denen
man Welten erschafft.
Einzig aber die Liebe
gibt uns dazu

die Kraft.4

Indeed--
to change ourselves
we need powers
with which worlds are created.
But only love
gives us the power
for this.

An East German reader will readily identify "the powers with which worlds are created" with the Communist movement. The words recall frequently heard rhetoric about the ability "to change the world." The idea that love can accomplish this comes up repeatedly in East German poetry. This is, I believe, part of the Romantic heritage of Marxism.

Most of Kahlau's poems are so simple in their language and didactic intent that analysis is rendered almost useless. One of the very few poems which can bear some extended probing is "Die Liebe muß sein!" Highly Brechtian in the ambivalence concealed under its deceptively placid surface, this poem gives a good example of how political messages can be slipped by in a highly controlled society:

DIE LIEBE MUß SEIN!

Die Liebe muß sein, sagten die Leute.

Die Liebe ist stärker als alles, sagten die Leute,
denn schließlich, sagten die Leute,

war die Liebe immer schon da.
Und also, sagten die Leute:
Die Liebe wird immer sein.
Aber die Liebe wird unterdrückt!
sagten die Leute,
die Liebe muß sich verstecken,
die Liebe hat Angst, sagten die Leute.
Das darf man der Liebe nicht antun!
sagten die Leute,
und haben die Liebe befreit!

Jetzt gibt es ein Land,
wo die Liebe gesiegt hat,
da macht jetzt die Liebe die Gesetze,
denn die Liebe hat zu bestimmen
über die Leute.
Nun gilt von Montag bis Sonntag
nur noch die Liebe,
und jetzt sagen die Leute, im Namen der Liebe:
Es gibt nur eine einzige, richtige, wahre Liebe,
und die haben wir!
Wer unsre Liebe nicht will, verdient keine Liebe!
Es gibt keine andere Liebe mehr in der Welt.

Die Liebe muß sein, flüstern die Leute.5

LOVE MUST PREVAIL!

Love must prevail, the people said.

Love is stronger than anything, the people said,
because really, the people said,
love was always there.
And therefore, the people said:
Love will always be there.
But love is oppressed!
the people said,
love has to hide,
love is afraid, the people said.
That must not be done to love!
the people said,
and they set love free!

Now there is a land
where love is victorious,
there the laws are now made by love,
because love has to rule
over the people.
From Monday to Sunday
all that counts is love,
and now the people say, in the name of love:
There is only a single, correct, true love,
and that is ours!
Whoever doesn't want our love doesn't deserve any love!
There is no longer any other love in the world.

Love must prevail, the people whisper.

The setting free of love is obviously intended to refer to the
proletariat revolution. One key word is "oppressed" (unterdrückt)
which is hardly used outside a political context.

Had Kahlau merely wanted to write one more hymn of praise to the revolution, he might have ended the poem in the middle. Instead, there is a second half, describing a development which seems diametrically opposite to the first. A bit of parody was already present in the first part of the poem, simply by virtue of the parable being so simplistic. The constant repetition of "the people said" adds a note of humor. It is like a political slogan, repeated so frequently that it begins to lose all meaning. In the second part, the parody becomes more apparent with every line, as the platitudes are piled up to the point of absurdity. In the third line of the second half we learn that there are still laws, an indication that perhaps love is not fully in control after all. This long stanza ends with an apparent denial of love. Finally, the last line of the poem echoes the beginning in an ironic twist. The statement that "love must prevail" was originally only an expression of hope. Now it is simultaneously a cry of despair. Attention is called to the word "whisper," the only change in what is otherwise an exact repetition of the first line. The difference between speech and whispering summarizes the entire development that has taken place. We are now back where we started, only the initial statement is made, out of fear, a bit less openly. The repetition suggests a cyclical pattern. Perhaps another revolution will be necessary? The voice of the people became stronger and more confident at first, later hesitant and weak. Except for the verb tense, it would be possible to move the last line of the poem to the beginning without disturbing the poem's coherence.

What this would at first seems to suggest is, at the very least, a severe rejection of the Communist revolution and, by implication, the East German government. While Kahlau has sometimes been critical of its policies, particularly with respect to the restrictions placed on writers, there is no doubt that he is fundamentally sympathetic to the state. It would probably be best to say that the poem is intended as a parable with a certain applicability to East Germany, not an actual description of the country. The necessity of disguising his message prevented Kahlau from adding qualifications. To communicate the critique at all, it was necessary to over-simplify. For Kahlau and probably the majority of his readers, the basic correctness of the Socialist system is simply taken for granted. There was little chance of such a critique being taken overly seriously.

East German critics have had no difficulty in recognizing the land in question as their own. Remarkably, they seem to have overlooked the irony entirely. Eva and Hans Kaufmann write:

> Seldom has a writer so unequivocally adopted the theory of no conflicts as Kahlau. The world has arrived...and so all that remains for the poet is the assignment to turn the heads of those who do not yet see this. Starting from this self-certainty, Kahlau sets problems in the poem that are always smoothly resolved and whose results set the "I" of the poem at ease. The prevailing rationality and sober understanding, for which there are no open problems left... hardly allow the possible greatness and totality of a love-relationship to appear believable.[6]

They simply assume that Kahlau's poem was intended as a literal description of the GDR. It seems peculiar that the Kaufmanns always extremely mild in their criticism of East German society, should make such a charge. It is no doubt the habit of accepting hymns of praise to the GDR uncritically which makes them blind to Kahlau's irony. Read in such a way, the poem becomes a sequence of cliches beyond what even the most uncritical bureaucrat could accept, something that would hardly be in character for a writer of Kahlau's quality.

The Kaufmanns are not the only ones to have completely overlooked this irony. In replying to the Kaufmanns, Rudolf Dau only pointed out that other books by Kahlau do not present relationships between the sexes as free of conflict. Dau nevertheless agrees that Kahlau, in the book Du, labored under the illusion that love was the only ruler in East Germany.[7] These critics support their case solely by citing the poem under discussion. Even if we forget the ample evidence in the poem which contradicts this thesis, the rest of the volume would not bear out such a conclusion. The poems express not only harmony but also fear, shyness, pity, surprise, confusion and occasionally even a slight touch of despair. With other writers as well, the Kaufmanns have often showed themselves insensitive to irony and ambiguity. I think it is conceivable that Dau may be recognizing the irony yet pretending not to. By being able to spot such a criticism, one comes close to sharing it. Dau may have felt it better to say nothing, avoiding embarrassment to Kahlau and himself.

Nevertheless, there are elements in Kahlau's book that help encourage such misinterpretations. Though conflicts are presented, they never seem to be taken very seriously. The book moves on a remarkably low level of intensity. "Die Liebe muß sein!" may actually be a bit of self-criticism.

The book closes with a section entitled "Alltägliche Lieder von Liebe," little episodes from everyday life put into verse. Among the poems in the series which best expresses Kahlau's ideal is the fifth:

Mein Mann? Ob ich ihn liebe?
Du, ich weiß es nicht.

Er war auf keinen Fall mein Ideal.
Das hat sich so ergeben
durch die Arbeit.
Als Mann war er mir vorher schnurzegal.
Er war sehr hilfsbereit
und furchtbar sachlich--
so wie er jetzt noch ist--
ja, auch zu Haus.
Du, der macht alles,
wenn ich Spätschicht habe.
Auch Trockenlegen
macht ihm gar nichts aus.
Ja, meine Eltern waren sehr dagegen--
die wollen ihn
bis heute noch nicht sehn.
Doch, er wird akzeptiert
von den Kollegen.
Mach's gut--da steht mein Mann!
Auf Wiedersehn![8]

My husband? Do I love him?
My, I don't know.
At any rate, he wasn't my ideal.
It's just a thing that happened
where we work.
He hadn't meant a thing to me till then.
He always tried to help
and was so practical
just as he is today--
yes, at home as well.

My, he does it all
when I must work at night.
Even the diapers
don't bother him
Yes, my parents were very much opposed--
they do not want
to see him even now.
Still, he is accepted
by our colleagues.
Enough--there is my husband!
Now good-bye!

Here we find the familiar East German theme of work forging a
bond between people. Lovers who first meet at the place of work
is something of a cliche in GDR literature. The public realm,
here represented by the colleagues, is given somewhat more
importance than the home. The woman's implicit answer to the
initial question is that of course she loves her husband.
Kahlau's ideal, like that of so many East German writers, is that
of a love so completely integrated into the pattern of everyday
life that it almost ceases to possess an independent identity.
The persistent use of understatement seems to suggest that a love
which must dramatize itself is somehow false. The poem may at
first seem like a spontaneous sketch drawn from everyday life. In
actuality, it is an idyll. Only the idyll's comparative unfam-
iliarity gives it an appearance of realism.

The last poem is a sort of epigram:

Die Liebe ist kein Zauberstab,
der jeden Wunsch erfüllt.
In jeder Liebe bleibt ein Teil
der Träume ungestillt.

Wer alles will, was Liebe kann,
der ist am End allein.
Die Liebe zwischen Frau und Mann
kann nie vollkommen sein.

Auf beide kommt es dabei an,
zu viel geht nur zu zwein.
Die Liebe zwischen Frau und Mann
muß Menschenliebe sein.[9]

Love is not a magic wand
to do what you have willed.
In every love you find a part
of dreams, yet unfulfilled.

Who asks love for the moon and stars
will lead a lonely life.
There always is a flaw that mars
the love of man and wife.

Two human beings are not enough
to leave the rest behind,
but need, in love of man and wife,
The love of humankind.

This poem, most especially the final two lines, summarizes the entire message of the book. It is an attempt to harmonize sexual love between two people with the more comprehensive demands of a larger society.

Mathilde Dau, an East German critic has said in reviews of Kahlau's book:

> The new love poems of Heinz Kahlau, which this time fill their own volume, are not only embodied private experience. They show the human--and that also means: not free of contradictions--face of a society that noticeably allows its possibilities for the development of creative individuals to become real, in which the most individual and the public spheres of life no longer have to appear separated from one another. The poems have this advantage over all later bourgeois love poetry.10

But how well are the private and public spheres really combined here? I am inclined to think that something in the former has been sacrificed. While there are excellent individual poems, the collection as a whole leaves me unsatisfied. The low key is not only monotonous but also unrealistic. There are no poems which communicate any real intensity. We are often charmed but never really moved. In the course of a person's life, more violent feelings will generally surface at least occasionally and will be present, somewhere beneath the surface, nearly always.

CHAPTER VII

GÜNTER KUNERT'S <u>INNOCENCE</u> <u>OF</u> <u>NATURE</u>:
THE USE OF PARODY

Parody is often the final stage in the development of a literary
movement. Even as Romanticism was established in Germany, it
became the object of affectionate parody for writers such as
Brentano and Hoffmann. As the Romantic movement drew to a close,
parody became the dominant mode, the best example being the early
songs of Heine. Authors were able to continue the Romantic
tradition by making fun of it. They perpetuated Romanticism, even
when this was only as a means of orientation.

A major difficulty confronting writers in the West is their
extreme lack of opposition. Because the prevalent values are so
nebulous, it is difficult to establish the sort of distinctive
identity known as style. Everything is absorbed into a sentimental eclecticism. Ideals tend to be so ill-defined as to
elude criticism. In this respect, writers in the Communist world
are at an advantage. Even when they may be persecuted, it is at
least some consolation to be taken seriously. The existence of a
prevailing ideology adds meaning to their work, regardless of
whether they support this or oppose it. There is a productive
tension that is lacking in the West.

Günter Kunert is perhaps the first East German writer of importance whose use of the prevailing ideology is primarily through parody. Born in 1929, he became a protege of Johannes R. Becher, but his style contrasts strikingly with the declamatory manner of his sponsor. John Flores has pointed out that Kunert's poems even "seem to have been written in direct opposition to the elevated, rhetorical sentiments of Becher's hymns to his recovered homeland and to the artificial 'Classicism' of his late sonnet cycles."[1]

More interesting, though elusive, are comparisons with Brecht, under whom Kunert also studied. The extreme simplicity of Kunert's language gives his poems a great superficial similarity to those of Brecht, which, however, only serves to highlight vast spiritual differences. Marcel Reich-Ranicki has pointed out that, while irony is Kunert's favorite literary device, "it is never mocking or cynical, it doesn't wound, it's purpose is far more to name and clarify phenomena."[2] That is something that certainly could not be said of Brecht. Lutz Rathenow considers Kunert to be intellectually far more penetrating than Brecht, without the latter's tendency to simplistic lessons or morals.[3] This view is, in essence, similar to the analysis of Fritz J. Raddatz, who points out that with Kunert, unlike Brecht, the poems end with the final line, not with an additional, unspoken stanza.[4] One could even say, with only a relatively small oversimplification, that Kunert genuinely is the sort of rationalistic poet Brecht only imagined himself to be.

While some GDR poets have tended toward rhetoric and extravagant daydreams, Kunert has cultivated stoicism and linguistic austerity. Beginning with a qualified optimism, he has taken an increasingly bleak view of the future,[5] culminating finally in a repudiation of any hope.[6]

Though the realism and sobriety of a poet like Kunert can be of immense value in a land saturated with grandiose illusions, it also carries with it certain spiritual dangers. In poems such as "Laika,"7 Kunert has been able to produce powerful warnings of the immanent destruction that could await our species, but the simple act of admonishing presupposes at least hope for improvement. Poetry requires, if not illusions, at least a certain capacity for enthusiasm. Flores finds the pessimism of Kunert's later poems "overbearing."8 Rathenow qualifies considerable admiration, only by observing that Kunert does not always avoid self-pity.9

The very idea of love poetry from such an author may strike us as paradoxical. Kunert manifests apparently little susceptibility to emotional intoxication. Kunert has not, in fact, produced a vast quantity of love poetry, yet it does fill one remarkable volume of his entitled Unschuld der Natur: 52 Figurationen leibhafter Liebe (Innocence Of Nature: 52 Variations on Physical Love). Many of the poems contained there must be ranked among Kunert's best. The emotional power of such a subject allows for few traces of the aridity which, elsewhere, is a danger in Kunert's poetry. Here as well, however, Kunert generally maintains a certain emotional distance. Most of his poems are written in the third person. Even in those poems which are not, there is something almost clinical in the objectivity with which Kunert describes emotions.

Kunert's love poetry is distinguished from virtually all the rest produced in East Germany by its use of physical imagery. There are few authors in any country who effectively make use of explicit sexuality. Kunert manages to avoid the self-conscious quality which so often accompanies such attempts, probably because his language is so austere. There is little of the sexual boasting that is found in such writers as Henry Miller or

Charles Bukowski. The poems are accompanied by rather realistic
drawings by Fritz Cremer, which show few traces of either
idealization or pornography. The illustrations highlight an
undertone of sadness in the poems, even when these appear to
glory in bodily existence.

A somewhat brutal sensuality is found in the title poem:

UNSCHULD DER NATUR

Die abgefallnen feuchten Blätter von den Birken
zerdrückte sie mit ihrem Hintern fest und weiß
derweil da einer sich auf ihr vergnügte
so selbstvergessen und gewärtig ihres Schreis

und voller Ungeduld daß der schon käme
aus ihrem lustversunkenen gewalkten Leib
unsäglich tönend aus bewußtseinsfernen Tiefen
wo Fleisch bloß ist des Fleisches Zeitvertreib.10

INNOCENCE OF NATURE

The moist leaves that had fallen from the birches
were pressed against her bottom, hard and white
Meanwhile, upon her, someone took his pleasure
knew just her cry, forgetting himself quite

and was impatient, suddenly to find
it left her body, full of lust and blows
strangely sounding from without the mind
where flesh on flesh is all the body knows.

The experience is summarized at the start of the second stanza
with the rather surprising word "impatient" (voller Ungeduld),
suggesting disappointment. The use of the third person and a
rather mechanical poetic form conspire to create an impression of
almost clinical detachment. The contrast between the violence of
the description and prosaic tone, corresponding to the gap
between mind and body, gives the poem a certain complexity. The
word "innocence" in the title may be partly ironic. Nature is
viewed as somewhat threatening and, in ways, not so innocent at
all.

One poem that seems especially to parody literature of the
GDR is "Wir waren zwei":

WIR WAREN ZWEI

Zwei Kolben einer Maschine
waren wir
bewegt im gleichen Takt.

Zwei Patronen in einer Kammer
abgeschossen auf das gleiche Ziel.

Zwei Räder waren wir
an einem Wagen
kannten nur die gleiche Umdrehung.

Dann zerfiel die Maschine dann
verrostete der Abzugsbügel zerbrach
die Achse.

Was kann noch kommen

als armes Flickwerk?

Schmeltzt uns ein
Mich und sie.11

WE WERE TWO

Pistons on a machine
keeping
the same time.

Two bullets in a chamber
shot at the same target.

We were two wheels
of a wagon
knowing only the same turns.

Then the machine broke down then
the trigger-guard rusted the axle
broke.

What is left
but dull repairs?

Melt us down.
Her and me.

The first verse satirizes the attempts at poeticizing of industry, strongly encouraged in the early days of the republic but never really successful. The second verse is a complex parody. The idea of lovers united by a common goal is, as we have seen, a familiar one in the Socialistic society of the GDR. It is to be found in several poems such as Becher's "Der gleiche Weg wie du." We have a sardonic play on words here, as the German word for "goal" (Ziel) can also mean "target." The two wheels turning together in the third verse could suggest changes in the party line.

In the fourth verse, the demolition comes quickly. Images of destruction are piled one on top of the other. There is an abrupt disillusionment. The rhythmic flow of the previous lines is broken, as though to suggest a malfunctioning machine. For the first time in the poem, the line breaks do not correspond to a natural pause. The final two lines may be read as a sort of epilogue. The directive to "Melt us down" is an ironic invitation to execute the speaker for his want of political enthusiasm. Cremer's illustration shows a woman gazing pensively at a mechanical figure sprawled on the ground in front of her.

Since the sixties, the relations of Kunert with the GDR cultural authorities had been strained.[12] Eventually, in 1980, after his books had been removed from stores and libraries, he would emigrate to the West.

CHAPTER VIII

VOLKER BRAUN'S "LOVE POEMS
FOR SUSANNE M. IN FLENSBURG":
THE DIALECTICAL PASSIONS

Volker Braun is a leading representative of the middle generation
of East German poets, but in many respects he is closer to the
poets who established themselves between the two world wars than
to his own contemporaries. For one thing, he is linked with the
Expressionists, the old revolutionaries and even the Nazis by a
radical cast of mind, a willingness to suggest unusual or extreme
solutions. There is a zealous enthusiasm in his work that is rare
among the younger poets. We find it when he sings the praises of
work or the promise of a new society. Such fervor is, however,
usually tempered by common sense and, even more, by a pervasive
irony. As with Thomas Mann and Bertolt Brecht, it is often
difficult to tell when he is joking and at whose expense. He is
not a master craftsman. Several of his compositions betray signs
of having been written too quickly, but his work shows, at its
best, a passionate intensity that is rare in contemporary
writing.

The poetry of Braun is usually characterized by the word "dialectic." I understand this term to mean any intellectual approach in which opposites are not regarded as mutually exclusive but rather as parts of a larger whole. To put it differently, truth is sought in the interplay of opposing principles, not in the exclusion of them. It is a mode of reasoning most closely identified with the Hegelian and Marxist traditions, yet by no means confined to them. The "Romantic irony" prophesied by Friedrich Schlegel might be described as dialectical, as it attempts to stand above all polarities, bound by neither time, space nor laws of reason. The poetry of Heine may be considered dialectical in that the author plays the passions and reason off against one another, locating truth only in the unresolved tension between these. So might the novels of Thomas Mann, who, in a less playful manner, traced the conflict between nature and spirit.

Braun, in accordance with the Marxist tradition, views dialectic fundamentally as a mode of reasoning, not as a poetic principle. He is striving to find a poetic equivalent of this logical approach. The poem, in other words, is to represent a synthesis of contradictory principles. Writing in a major East German student magazine, Hans Richter calls Braun "a historian among the younger poets" and describes the poetics of Braun in eminently Marxist terms. Braun's "speciality," according to Richter, has "become the dialectic of present (the past included) and future comprehended in the productive process."[1]

What this really means with respect to poetic technique is that Braun tries to combine the most divergent elements within his poetry. He frequently presents us with conflicting feelings or ideas. The focus switches between the present and the future, the ideal and the real. John Flores observes that Braun's "most impressive technique is the controlled shift of poetic gestures, the startling modulation in the speaker's tone of voice."[2] Thus we find elevated rhetoric juxtaposed with colloquialism, earnest appeals with irony and sarcasm, emphatic explanations with probing questions. The shifts in tone tend to be abrupt. Braun's verse is really dramatic rather than lyrical. It is deliberately inharmonious and frequently lacking in sensuous appeal. The drama that we find in his poems is not so much of conflict among men. Rather, it takes place in the theater of ideas. Highly intellectual but in a manner that is sometimes blunt to the point of crudeness, Braun follows the movement of human thought through all its changes and reversals.

What generally enables Braun to combine such disparate elements in a single poem is the use of strong rhythms and alliteration. By these means, we are swept along even when the shifts of tone or meaning might otherwise give us cause to hesitate. It is the music which generally provides the unity in his poems, even when the sense mitigates against this. When Braun fails, it is, as Richter has observed, frequently because he overloads his poetry, presenting elements so disconnected that even techniques such as the heavy use of alliteration can no longer give an impression of coherence.[3]

That Braun's poetic work is often stirring and powerful seems beyond question to me, but I find certain limitations inherent in his poetic method. The musical unity that Braun achieves within his poems tends to be only a sort of artificial synthesis, a matter of style rather than substance. Take away the linguistic devices and we find ourselves faced with practical decisions, it is generally necessary to mediate between opposites or choose among them. Their dramatic juxtaposition will not help us. We do not find a great deal of practical wisdom in Braun's work.

At the same time, the dialectical movement between extremes has the artistic advantage of providing a balance which allows the author to render passions in a condition of relatively unmitigated purity and intensity, something that is generally very difficult in view of the innumerable prosaic compromises necessitated by the modern world. In Braun's love poems we are most especially aware of this. They frequently show extremes of passion that are hardly to be found elsewhere in contemporary poetry, but, at the same time, this passion is never presented as an absolute. It is restrained, though not greatly diminished, by awareness of the larger social context. The best example of this is perhaps Braun's remarkable series "Liebesgedichte für Susanne M. in Flensburg":

LIEBESGEDICHTE FÜR SUSANNE M. IN FLENSBURG

I
Du fährst nachhaus: die Stadt fährt ab
Der Zug zerreißt ein Wölkchen Rauch

Was lieb mir ist zerbrichst du gern
Ich höre deine Stimme nur

Ich sehe deine Hände nur
Ich preise öffentlich dein Haar

Und vieles was dir heilig ist
Vernichte ich an jedem Tag

Bin ich von Liebe heiß, von Haß?
Zwei Monde hat die Nacht, gestehs!

Die Morde schweigst du ungetan
Auf Lippen übe ich Verrat

Du fährst nachhaus, dein Brief ist leer:
Nehmt Hände mir und Stimme weg!

Dochwenndusprichst: Ichliebedich!
Somußichweinenbitterlich--

LOVE POEMS FOR SUSANNE M. IN FLENSBURG

I
You travel home: the city fades
The train tears through a cloud of smoke

The things I love you like to break
I hear your voice and that is all

I see your hands and that is all
Publicly I praise your hair

And what for you are holy things
I destroy with every day

Am I hot with love, with hate?
Night has a double moon, confess!

You hush the murders up undone
On lips I practice to betray

You travel home, your letter blank:
You take my hand and voice away!

Butwhenyousay: Iloveyouso!
Mybittertearsbegintoflow--

II

UNÜBERLEGTER BRIEF NACH FLENSBURG

Ich sage dir nicht: du bist geschändet
Eh sie dich in die Werkhallen abschleppen, an
Fernschreiber fesseln, dir ihre Milch
Ihren Rundfunk angewöhnen, dich in
Hautenge Strümpfe stecken bis zum Zeh

Eh sie die helle Bucht der Schenkel
Aufbrechen, eh sie dich feiern, eh sie
Die süße Lüge in dich gießen
Eh du nach den Umarmungen blank und
Blödsinnig sorglos in die Reklame blinzelst

Eh du Kinder gebierst für die Armee der großen
Reklamemacher, Huren herstellst oder
Helden großziehst, die man tot
Beweinen wird--ich sage dir nicht:
Keine ist schlechter als du, Gutmütige!

Unterschiedlos ist die Stellung der Zähne im
Biß und im Ja der Vermählung: Nuancen
Retten nicht mehr: Verzweiflung wird als

Hingabe gewertet, Trauer als
Konzentration auf den Endsieg

Nichts mehr sag ich dir: jede Wahrheit
Verschweige ich, jedes Schweigen
Will ich ertragen: ich sage dir nicht mehr
Ich erwarte dich hier!
                    Unsere Liebe
Legen wir auf Montag nach dem Krieg.

II
UNCONSIDERED LETTER TO FLENSBURG

I will not tell you: you are disgraced
Until they drag you off in factories, fasten
You to telegraph machines, accustom you
To milk of their radio, stick you
In skin-tight stockings down to the toe

Until they break open the bright
Inlet of your thighs, until they
Pour sweet lies into you
Until after the embrace when you blink
Blank and stupidly content at neon signs

Until you bear children for the army of great
Advertisers, Producing whores or
Raising heroes, whose death
Will be mourned--I will not say
Nobody is worse than you, generous one!

No difference where the teeth are placed in
A bite and in the yes of betrothal: nuances
No longer save: despair is
Understood as devotion, sadness
As concentration on the final victory

I will tell you nothing more: every truth
I will keep secret: every silence
Shall be endured by me: I will not say
I await you here!
                    Our love
We set for Monday after the war.

III

ANMERKUNG FÜR BÜRGER DER DEUTSCHEN DEMOKRATISCHEN
REPUBLIK

Laßt keins der Häuser mehr träg
Herumstehn, grabt sie nicht zum Wegfauln ein
Laßt die Straßen nicht länger lustlos
Sielen im Regen sein, verbaumelt nicht in Gerüsten
Unsere Zeit, kleistert Stuck nicht, seid
Nie mehr verlegen vor euren Fäusten!
Laßt kein Stück Himmel blaß und nackt westwärts treiben.

Helft den Himmel mit Regenbogenfarben
Anfüllen, mit kreisenden Monden, laut
Von der Lust der Demonstrationen und Jahrmärkte
Schwer von Lärm tollender Häuserhorden, von

Festen der Milchkannen, Prozessionen der Kinderwagen
Hochgetrieben von Freude! Ihr, Maurer, Technologen:
Laßt kein Stück Himmel blaß und nackt westwärts treiben.

Laßt ihn westwärts ziehn: augfüllende Lockung,
Spiegel der Zukunft des Landes, vorbereitet
Noch den Atem zu betören im Mund, Regen-
Spritze ins trübe Herzblut, Verjagung
Aller Schwachheit: Bett konstruiert
Schlafende hinzuführen wo sie erwachen
Wo sie sich kennen, wo sie sich retten

Denn meine Liebe allein ist kein Beweis.[4]

III

NOTE TO CITIZENS OF THE GERMAN DEMOCRATIC REPUBLIC

Let no house stand idly around
Any more, entrenched till it decays
No longer let the streets be joyless
Gutters for rain, don't dawdle away our time
On scaffolding, don't paste on facades, no longer
Be embarrassed by your fists!
Let no bit of sky drift westward naked and pale.

Help the sky fill with rainbow
Colors, with circling moons, loud
With energy of fairs and demonstrations
Heavy with the noise of busy neighborhoods, from
The feast of milk cans, processions of cradles

Lifted up by joy! You, builders, engineers:
Let no bit of sky drift westward naked and pale.

Let it move westward: A tempting eye-full
Mirror of the future of the land, prepared
Still to fool the breath inside the mouth, a burst
Of rain in the dark heart's blood, purgation
Of all weakness: bed, constructed
To lead the sleepers where they will awaken
Where they know themselves, where they save themselve

For my love alone proves nothing.

The juxtaposition of disconnected ideas and images, so common in Braun's poetry, here effectively expresses a distraught state of mind. The series of poems concerns love across the border of the two Germanies, a girl who has abandoned her partner to live in the West. We must remember that this is in a country where close friends and even families were abruptly torn apart by the Berlin Wall in 1961, only five years before the publication of this poem, erected largely to prevent emigration of the intelligentsia. The area of travel and emigration is one in which the East Germans had been asked to accept considerable personal sacrifices for the sake of political ends. The theme chosen by Braun is therefore one surrounded by very intense personal and political emotions. The conflicts that he renders are those faced on some level by many citizens of his country. Braun, as we shall see, ultimately seems to give priority to the public sphere, by implication justifying the policy of the government, but only after showing the claims of personal life in their full intensity.

Already, in the first of the three poems, we have an intricate complex of conflicting emotions. Despite the loose
organization of the poem, a conflict between the personal and
private spheres is identifiable, especially in the third couplet.
Initially at least, Braun is not ready to give the social realm
priority. The speaker's life in society seems to be a facade,
behind which his true feelings must remain concealed. The last
two lines are a quote from a poem by Heine[5] run together, as if
a record were played at too high a speed and thereby transformed
into babble. Perhaps this is meant to indicate that the speaker
would like to close in a manner that, like that of Heine, is
witty and elegant, but that the conflicts are too serious to
allow for that.

The three poems describe stages in the recovery from a
shattered relationship. The initial emotional confusion gradually
takes on form. In the second poem, the conflicts and tensions
become more articulate. It tells us much about the intense
emotions that surround the issue of emigration on both sides of
the border. The political issues are here eroticized in a very
remarkable way. It is almost as if the Federal Republic itself
were an object of sexual jealousy. The speaker sees himself as a
representative of the GDR. It might be possible to read the
separation of the two lovers as an allegory on the divided
country. The nightmarish picture of the West in the first stanza
is, however, not intended to be an objective account. The word
"unconsidered" in the title cautions us against understanding
this too literally.

The driving force in this poem is the tension between love
and anger. The first stanza begins with a promise of forbearance,
a refusal to condemn Susanne. But, as this refusal is prolonged,
it begins to sound like a bitter rejection. That message, however, is also partially retracted by the praise at the end of

the third stanza. The love and anger are, I think, somewhat imperfectly fused in the last two stanzas. At the very end, the speaker resolves to mourn no longer. After the fourth stanza, the reader may anticipate a decision to follow Susanne and journey to the West. The last line of the poem, however, abruptly closes off the possibility of any immanent reconciliation, personal or political. It is hard to know exactly what the "war" is meant to refer to. To see a prophesy of a third world war here seems a bit extreme, but the speaker seems to at least suggest an irreconcilable conflict between East and West. It is a highly dramatic image, perhaps exaggerated but appropriate to a very excited frame of mind. Fritz J. Raddatz sees a number of echoes in the line, from Schwejk to Brecht's leave-taking from Lukacs.[6] The appointment is, in any case, absurd and ironic. It is a way of saying that the love will never be resumed, at any rate not until the world has been transformed completely.

The dialectical conflict between the public and private spheres, sustained through the first two poems, is not resolved in a higher synthesis. However reluctantly, it is the public sphere which is affirmed in the end. The violent feelings are to be sublimated in activity. Instead of personal satisfaction, the love shall help to build collective accomplishments.[7] This is, most especially, the meaning of the final line of the entire series. Because of what the speaker has sacrificed for them, the task of building a new society gains in urgency and importance. The happiness or unhappiness of the individual is finally assigned a subordinate role.

The last poem contains an idealized picture of the GDR that contrasts with Braun's frightening image of the Federal Republic. Both images are highly subjective and can be understood as hardly concealed projections of the author's wishes and fears. I do not, however, believe that the series of poems is basically political in it intent. It only appears so because, as might be expected in a Socialist country, the images used to embody the author's feelings are borrowed from the political realm.

The love affair across the border of the two Germanies takes on a special meaning in the context of East German ideology and propaganda. The Federal Republic is a mysterious entity with respect to which the East Germans define themselves, but about which very little is actually known. This makes it a convenient setting for their daydreams and nightmares. The vulgarity and wealth of the Federal Republic, both real enough, tend to be exaggerated. The official ideology establishes certain definite expectations for sexual love in both West and East. The relationship described in this series occupies a sort of indeterminate position not covered by the ideology. It exists almost outside the established framework, preserving an excitement and mystery which ideological rationalizations tend to diminish.

Braun seems to have an understandable need to distance himself from the highly emotional experiences expressed in this series. In a note to the poems, he says:

These odes idealize the weak love of my friend Dieter Dunger of Erfurt who struggled with separation at the difficult age of 22.[8]

I can only receive this with a bit of skepticism. The poems have several strong signs of autobiographical content. Without the note, it would hardly occur to the reader to think of them as anything else. For one thing, poems of vicarious or imagined experience are unlikely to achieve this intensity. Furthermore, such poems generally simplify the experience described. despite what Braun says, these poems do not actually "idealize" the love at all. They show it in many aspects. The author seems to be straining to capture feelings of such complexity that they fall almost outside the scope of literature. Especially in the first poem, many obscure lines sound as if they allude to something highly personal. Even if Braun is really speaking for a friend, there are surely autobiographical elements here as well. One may wonder if the note is designed to protect the author's personal life by throwing curious readers off the track. The emotionalism and obscurity of the poems make them something that could easily become material for a Romantic legend. By calling the account "idealized" and remarking on the immaturity of the speaker, Braun seems to be trying to avoid this.

Braun has only rarely achieved similar intensity in his subsequent work. One poem from a later collection entitled "Fastnachtsspaß" could, however, almost serve as a sequel to the series just discussed:

FASTNACHTSSPAß

Einmal im Jahr--
Wenn die frühlingsfrohen Pritschen
Auf des Winters kalte Tatzen
Schlagen, wenn ich die lachende
Maske trage dort, wo das Herz war
Wenn sich die Liebenden wiegen
Nicht achtend der vorlauten Gaslaterne:
Und ich weiß dich an eine Kleinbürgerbrust
Gelümmelt, und ich will nicht
Im dumpfen Dunkel quavoller
Selbstlust Lügen aufsuchen--

Einmal

Geh ich zu allen meinen Freundinnen
Endlich zu klären: jene ist die Einzige
Die ich je lieben werde

Und sie halten es
Für Spaß[9]

CARNIVAL PRANK

Once a year--
When the joyous blows of Spring
Strike the chilly paws
Of Winter, when I wear the laughing
Mask, there, where the heart has been
When lovers cradle each other
Ignoring the bold lantern by the curb:
And I know you tarry on the breast of
A philistine, and I do not wish
To seek for lies within the dull
Dark of tormented complaisance--

Once
I go to all my girlfriends
To explain at last: she is the only one
That I will ever love

And they take it
For a joke.

The climax of the poem comes in the fourteenth and fifteenth lines with a declaration of love stronger than most contemporary poets, even with the distancing effect of irony, would be likely to make. The remainder of the poem may be seen as a sort of frame which renders this emotionally and artistically possible. It is difficult today to give such a statement even the appearance of plausibility. If the reader believes, or almost believes, it here, that is because the girlfriends do not. The reaction of disbelief has been anticipated, thus making it difficult for the reader to assume. The tension builds steadily through the first twelve lines, to a point where something very drastic is anticipated. We have a degree of melodrama not often found in contemporary writing.[10] After such a build-up, lines thirteen through fifteen might impress the reader as slightly comic. But, in the last two lines, the joke is turned around. The friends, and perhaps the reader as well, turn out to be the hypocrites.

It is possible to see a larger social commentary in the poem. The utterances which express our deepest feelings have become so abused that they can no longer be taken seriously. Honesty has become impossible. As is frequently the case, one wonders whether Braun realizes himself what a harsh picture of East German society he is presenting. The solution offered in "Liebesgedichte für Susanne M. in Flensburg" no longer seems possible. The life in society can offer no consolation for personal unhappiness. Identification with it is a sham. We can begin to sense a crisis in Socialist literature and ideology.

Braun's later work has tended to be increasingly less declamatory than his first book, from which the poem to Susanne M. is taken. Braun himself maintains that the "blind" optimism of his earlier work, though not actually diminished, has been tempered by a greater appreciation of historical and social complexities. This, he remarks, is responsible for the "elegiac, cynical, bitter tones against the contemporary stagnation."[11] It might be possible to explain such outbursts of near despair as merely movements in a dialectical process, to be comprehended only in the context of a larger whole. His expressions of optimism, however, do not seem to convey a comparable intensity.

CHAPTER IX

SARAH KIRSCH: A FEMININE PERSPECTIVE

It is curious to compare the prominence that women in the GDR have achieved in fiction with their comparative lack of recognition in the area of lyric poetry. Anna Seghers, Christa Wolf, Irmtraut Morgner and other female novelists have achieved a status that very few of their masculine counterparts can equal. Among lyric poets of the GDR, only Sarah Kirsch approaches having a comparable position.

Although Christa Wolf has distanced herself from many Western forms of Feminism, she has constantly attempted, in a deliberate and systematic manner, to render a female perspective in her works.[1] That the cadences and ideas in the poetry of a woman should be different from those rendered by a man is not necessarily something to be taken for granted. The tone of Sarah Kirsch's poetry, however, is distinctly feminine. Sarah Kirsch differs from Christa Wolf in her lack of interest in theoretical constructs. She does not appear to proceed from any explicit viewpoint about the relationship between literature and society.

Sarah Kirsch's reluctance to discuss the theoretical foundation of her poetry is plainly not due to any intellectual
inadequacy. Not only her poems, but also stories and interviews,
make it clear that she is a highly articulate individual. The
refusal is a conscious choice, a means of preserving a certain
artistic autonomy.

In 1962 the youth magazine Forum put a series of questions
to a number of poets, among which was the following: "Does the
new position of people in a Socialist society, particularly as it
is brought about by the technical revolution, lead to any change
in the structure and content of lyric poetry?" Sarah Kirsch
responded to this, as to the other questions, by dismissing it as
irrelevant:

> For at least three years I have gotten used to the necessary
> absence of important economic questions in my poems. I am
> content with the edges of clouds, silver birds, silver
> sharks, work-hall dinosaurs (those are machines), the crests
> of antennas, t.v. screens, the neon crests of swans and all
> of those other things in whose actualization I can play no
> part. Now I leave the technical revolution to its own
> devices and do not (apart from reading newspapers, opening
> my eyes when appropriate) concern myself with it, thinking
> that if I need the technical revolution it will appear in my
> lines, hopefully rendered in such a way that scholars will
> recognize it at once and find no opportunity for marginal
> notes....I am also not certain whether the position of people
> in society has changed so much through the technical rev-
> olution and, if so, whether this will have any immediate
> effect on lyric poetry.[2]

The reply is typical of Sarah Kirsch's casual attitude toward theoretical debates.

This attitude can often be refreshing in the ideologically charged world of GDR poetry, but it places a larger burden of responsibility on the reader for his correct or mistaken interpretations. Sarah Kirsch has often emphasized her desire not to restrict the reader overly much, to leave him a little "room for play" (Spielraum) of the imagination.

Early in her career, Sarah Kirsch was influenced by more aggressively ideological poets such as Maurer and Mayakovski, but her mature work seems written in direct opposition to their manner. This poetry has no place for melodrama. The imagery does not usually range very far from the realm of common experience. The very simplicity of Sarah Kirsch's poetry makes it difficult to analyze. Her voice is neither the solitary "I" of most traditional lyric poetry nor the public, declamatory style employed by poets like Mayakovski, Becher and, at times, Maurer. It is private but not isolated, as if she were speaking to a lover, a close friend or an intimate circle.

Perhaps the most fundamental way in which the poetry of Sarah Kirsch differs from that of her early mentors is in the blending of emotions in her work. The mood of Maurer is frequently ecstatic, occasionally despairing, but almost always easily definable. Sarah Kirsch, somewhat more realistically, tends to fuse several emotional elements in her work. Joy and sadness, whimsy and seriousness almost always accompany one another. At the same time, the word "ironic" seems inappropriate. Irony lies in the tension between various meanings expressed simultaneously in a single phrase or statement. in the work of Sarah Kirsch one finds, it is true, ambiguities, but the meanings do not seem to be in conflict.

All writing, particularly poetry, is a process of abstraction, whereby experience is simplified. Every moment contains sensations and intuitions that are both too numerous and too elusive to be recorded fully. In this sense, poetry must always stand apart from life and any attempt at realism is partial at best. Criticism, since it uses literature and not raw experience as its point of departure, is necessarily on a still higher plane of abstraction. It attempts to classify and describe analytically the material which the poet has already filtered from the chaos of experience. It is the critic's job to carve stones which the poet has brought up from the earth. Poetry and criticism, in other words, are different stages in a single process of abstraction.

This abstraction is an ambivalent affair. It is necessary for society in the purest practical way. We must process experience in order to be able to deal with it rationally. From this point of view, art is anything but a luxury. Nevertheless, the abstraction is necessarily also a process of falsification. It involves choices which appear arbitrary with respect to both form and content. From Plato on, writers have frequently expressed doubts about poetry, on both moral and intellectual grounds. I think of another important female poet, the American Marianne Moore, who began her famous lyric entitled "Poetry" with the words "I too dislike it."

This is not the place for me to elaborate at length on the philosophical implications of the act of writing. I wish only to identify the ambivalence felt by many practitioners, particularly as this relates to the work of Sarah Kirsch. While all poetry involves the processing of experience, she seems to wish to minimize this. Her work is characterized by the juxtaposition of many contraries: man and nature, sadness and ecstasy, innocence and experience. Nevertheless, there is no self-conscious attempt to harmonize opposites, such as one finds in the work of many German authors such as Schiller, Thomas Mann or Volker Braun. The contraries appear never to have been separated. The style, unlike that of Braun, is not based on a dialectical process. Put another way, Sarah Kirsch does not tend to break down moods into their composite emotions.

The poetry of Sarah Kirsch is of an elemental sort which does not lend itself to criticism. In a country where writers have always tended to become obsessed with theoretical prescriptions, she tries to preserve, as much as possible, the integrity of pure experience. As Sarah Kirsch has remarked in the already quoted reply to Forum, she wishes her poetry to provide few occasions for marginal notes. Her work, in sum, remains deliberately at a comparatively low level of abstraction.

The poems of Sarah Kirsch can seldom be easily identified as belonging to any recognized genre or style. She has, however, said of her collection Rückenwind (Wind at my Back): "But when you read such a book, completely at your ease and under no pressure-- not because the poems are a subject of discussion--I believe that you will gradually notice that it consists largely of love poems."[3] The example she gives is the following:

DER WALD

Motorsägen heulen.
Wo Schatten war, Himmel.
Tag- und Nachtgestirn. Die zärtlichen Moose Perlgras,
Schlafmohn und Thymian
Fragen warum denn
Immer nur mein Fuß?[4]

THE WOOD

Electric saws screech.
Where shadow was, sky.
Stars of the day and night. The delicate mosses
Pearl-grass, poppies and thyme
Asking why is it
Always my foot alone?

As Sarah Kirsch intends the poem to be read, the emphasis in the final line is on the possessive pronoun. The final question might be rephrased as: "Why do you always go here alone?" She goes so far as to deny the validity of alternative interpretations.[5]

The images in the initial four lines convey a contrast between nature, represented by the vegetation, and society, represented by the electric saws. Characteristically, however, instead of looking for a symbolic resolution of the dichotomy, Sarah Kirsch concludes the poem by shifting the focus to a personal response.

It is far easier to recognize the intensely feminine quality of Sarah Kirsch's poetry than to say exactly in what this consists. Such analysis is particularly difficult at this historical juncture, since it appears that humanity may now be in the process of reinterpreting the significance of gender. Still, this femininity is something that informs Sarah Kirsch's poetry so completely that one is not likely to understand the work apart from it. I will therefore offer a few suggestions, bearing in mind that, as with all such broad characterizations, considerable simplification is inevitable.

The feminine principle has throughout history been identified with the earth, with a mother goddess who stands in
contrast with the male deity who rules the sky. The feminine
tends further to be identified with vegetation and agriculture,
as opposed to the more masculine world of hunting. The domestic
world--the home--is traditionally considered the feminine realm.
The worlds of war and commerce are considered masculine. I wish
only to point out these associations. I am not concerned with
whether they are cultural or inborn, still less do I wish to
become involved with such speculative discussions as whether
society once went through a matriarchal stage.

The feminine quality of Sarah Kirsch's poetry lies at least
in part in its closeness to the earth. It lies in the preference
for familiar, domestic imagery, in the desire to protect the
integrity of experience from the encroachments of theory. Take
the following poem:

BEKANNTSCHAFT

Guten Tag, Kamm!
Willst du
nicht bei mir bleiben,
daß ich immer schön bin?

Guten Tag, Katze,
willst du
nicht bei mir bleiben?
Du bist lustig
tanzt auf zwei Beinen.

Guten Tag, Lieber,
willst du

nicht bei mir bleiben?
Ich bin schön
und kann lachen.[6]

ACQUAINTANCE

Good morning, comb!
Don't you
want to stay with me,
so I will always be pretty?

Good morning, cat,
don't you
want to stay with me?
You are funny,
dance on two legs.

Good morning, love,
don't you
want to stay with me?
I am pretty
and can laugh.

There is something of the common-sense practicality here that one finds in the work of many important female poets such as Dickinson, Droste-Hülshoff, Moore or Akhmatova.

In her comments on Feminism, Sarah Kirsch has tended to take a negative view. She has said, for example: "I am on no account concerned with female emancipation, as has sometimes been claimed. I consider writing of emancipation to be nonsense. Men

and women should be united rather than set against one another..."[7] Such sentiments are likely to impress those living
in the West as conservative. They may appear surprising coming
from author who--together with such figures as Elke Erb, Christa
Wolf, Irmtraut Morgner and others--has contributed so much to a
literature of and, to a large extent, for women.[8] The statement
is, however, in line with the views of such female Socialists as
Rosa Luxemburg and Clara Zetkin. To appreciate the position of
Sarah Kirsch in context, it is well to remember that GDR society
places less emphasis on the atomic individual than is customary
in the West. The basic unit of society is less the individual
than the family.[9]

During the seventies and early eighties, the Feminist movement in North America and Western Europe worked to reduce the
importance of sexual roles in society. During this same period
women of the GDR, and probably other countries of Eastern and
Central Europe as well, have also become increasingly conscious
of their social position. Rather than denigrate the importance of
gender, however, they have usually sought to define this more
humanely. Typical is the October 1982 petition to East German
head of state Erich Honecker, signed by about 300 women, in
protest against new laws that provided for female conscription in
the event of a national emergency. The signatories repeatedly
emphasize that they are speaking specifically as women. They view
themselves as having "a special duty to protect life, to support
the old, the sick, and the weak." They see military service as
"...a contradiction of their womanhood."[10] Out of the petition
grew Women for Peace, the only organization within the independent peace movement in the GDR to operate on an almost
national scale. Those who see a suggestion of passivity in the
emphasis placed on the separate role of women should consider the
courage shown by the signatories of the petition when faced with
arrest and possible prosecution.

This sort of female solidarity in the GDR represents, of course, no more of a monolithic movement than does Feminism in the West. It is conceivable that, in the perspective of history, the difference between the two developments may one day seem rather small, but they certainly do not emphasize the same concerns. In East Germany the female solidarity has usually taken fairly undramatic and unpolitical forms, but the treatment that cultural authorities have sometimes accorded its representatives suggests that this development is perceived as a threat to the existing society. Despite the size of her public, Christa Wolf has had difficulty with the distribution of her work. Her books are published in the GDR, but the editions are not commensurate with her reputation.[11] Sarah Kirsch, also immensely popular, lived in increasing tension with the GDR cultural authorities. She eventually emigrated to the West in 1977, in the aftermath of Wolf Biermann's expulsion.

CHAPTER XI

LUTZ RATHENOW: THE PATTERN REVERSED

The founding of the GDR was accompanied by an emotional intoxication. The prevailing tone of most literature was one of
extreme optimism. Georg Maurer, for example, viewed such optimism
as one essential feature which distinguished recent GDR poetry
from that of the Federal Republic.[1] The authors were not simply
motivated by a desire to conform to the official doctrine of
Socialist Realism. The optimism was also a reaction to the
traumas of the previous decade. The German defeat in World War II
created a desire to break with the past, leaving behind a period
of hardship, guilt and humiliation. People, in others words, were
forced to believe strongly in the future, because the past and
the present could inspire so little respect.

   Gradually, however, melancholy tones appeared in the work of
important lyricists, most notably Johannes Bobrowski and Peter
Huchel. In the work of Günter Kunert one can even, as we have
seen, encounter expressions of deep pessimism. Hans-Dietrich
Sander has given us an extensive account of the gradual postponement of the utopian vision designated as "Communism."[2]
Since 1917, though no timetable was ever firmly enunciated, it

was generally believed that the transition from Socialism to Communism was something that already living generations would experience.[3] Doubts about such an imminent transformation eventually spread to the Communist party itself. In 1967 Walter Ulbricht, following Soviet precedents, declared in a speech that "Socialism is not a short-lived transitional period in the development of society but arelatively independent social-economic formation in the historical epoch of the transition from Capitalism to Communism on a world scale."[4] A transformation which appeared so remote could not easily console people for present difficulties.

Transcendence, in general, has not been a major concern of Communist literature. Suffering has tended to be viewed as something to be overcome, not endured or made acceptable. Brecht, for example, wished to avoid any catharsis that might come through identification with a hero. But suffering, insofar as it continues, is thus deprived of all meaning. Viewed as something accidental, it becomes far more acute.[5] As confidence in the future waned, it became inevitable that the longing for transcendence, a fundamental part of the poetic impulse, should reassert itself.

In a country where the state is as all-encompassing as in East Germany, it is hard to exclude the political dimension from any artistic expression, love poetry included. Some of the poets we have looked at have tried, often rather self-consciously, to view sexual love as an anticipation of a perfected world. As the confidence in this utopia, perhaps never really very secure to begin with, faded, it became necessary to reinterpret the experience. In the love poetry of Lutz Rathenow, we find an almost complete reversal of this conception. The future is viewed with more fear than longing. Love appears as a real if qualified transcendence, a respite from the anxiety that is pervasive. His poems celebrate brief moments of peace in a generally threatening world.

Born in 1952, Rathenow belongs to a generation of oppositional writers in the GDR that has risen to an early prominence, filling a gap in a literary community that was decimated by the emigration of so many leading figures, among them Wolf Biermann, Günter Kunert, Reiner Kunze and Sarah Kirsch. Rathenow studied literature and history at the University of Jena, but, in 1976, was forced to withdraw three months before graduation for his participation in a protest against the expulsion of singer-songwriter Biermann. He then moved to East Berlin, where he supported himself with a series of temporary jobs, while becoming established as a free-lance writer. There he was a founder of a private literary circle which sponsored readings in homes without official sanction. His work appeared only occasionally in East German magazines, but his reputation was established largely through work published abroad. In 1980 he was briefly arrested for using a West German publisher, Ullstein Verlag, for a book of his stories entitled Mit dem Schlimmsten wurde schon gerechnet (Prepared for the Worst). He was released from prison after only ten days, but contintued to lead a rather precarious existence. His home was searched and many books were confiscated. For a time, agents were stationed outside his home and he was interrogated almost daily. As of this writing, his circumstances have improved considerably, but his fate remains unpredictable.

Rathenow's entire career has been on the fringes of the established literary community and has flourished in an uneasy peace with the authorities. The poems we will look at were written primarily in the two years leading up to his arrest and are touched by an anticipation of a possible immanent disaster.

The following is among his earlier poems:

ENTSCHULDIGEN BITTE

Ich werde nicht zärtlich sein, kann nicht still
und zurückhaltend lieben. Zwei Hände greifen
dich an Lippen zerwühlen den Schlaf
deines Körpers. Ich werde rücksichtslos sein
bis in deinen Mund bricht das Schweigen, ein Stöhnen
ansetzt überrollt unser Zimmer. Beben
beginnen, die Welt umkippt[6]

EXCUSE ME PLEASE

I will not be tender, cannot be still
and reserved in love. Two hands grasp
at you, lips mangle the sleep
of your body. I will be ruthless
until the silence breaks inside your mouth, a moan errupts
to overroll the room. Tremors
begin, the world tips over

This poem shows a characteristic intensity but is, nevertheless, immature in its conception. The image of the earthquake comes very close to being trite, though the strong rhythm is almost enough to carry it. There is some residue here of that Communist tradition which associated sexual love with millennial expectations, especially the apocalyptic imagery in the last two lines. Rathenow seems to be experimenting. The apologetic title suggests an almost adolescent uncertainty, a lack of confidence with respect to both personal and literary matters. He has not yet discovered his own style, but a certain constellation of themes is starting to emerge. As in his later poetry, violence provides a background in relation to which the act of love is understood.

More typical of Rathenow's mature work is "Am Abend":

AM ABEND

Am Abend versammeln wir
unsere Hände Deine Finger nisten
in meinem Haar Die Worte räumen
den Mund: dies deutliche Fühlen
zwecklose Träumen--
               und
dein Körper wird leicht
bevor er herabstürzt[7]

AT EVENING

At evening we gather our hands
Your fingers nest in my hair
The words leave the mouth: This
clear feeling purposeless dreaming--
               and
your body grows light
before it plummets down

Surer and more original than "Entschuldigen bitte," this poem almost reverses the constellation of the earlier piece. Now it is the world that is violent. Rather than an explosion, love becomes a respite. This poem was sent to me by the author about a year before Rathenow's arrest, yet surely after arrangements for the publication of the book which provoked his arrest had been made. At the time I had a vague premonition that he might be in danger, but I was unable to evaluate the extent of this. Though the letters which he wrote to me were deceptively cheerful, this poem immediately filled me with a sense of foreboding. The intuition, at first half articulate, was confirmed by Rathenow's arrest.

Afterwards the poem, most especially the last line, constantly went through my mind. Of itself, the poem might be ambiguous. Taking the circumstances into account, however, an expectation of impending disaster in the final line seems clear. The violence of the verb at the end shocks us, especially by contrast with the gentler imagery of the previous lines. On one level it might refer to the descent into sleep, yet to describe sleep with such a harsh metaphor is unusual. The "dream-world" which lies ahead inspires fear. Now it is the present moment which must provide consolation.

In the same magazine as the previous poem, the following was also published:

AUCH EIN LIEBESGEDICHT

Wo wir standen, weiß ich noch
Es muß gegen Abend gewesen sein
Ich erinnere mich nicht, was du mir
was ich dir sagte. Ich weiß nicht
ob ich deine Hand hielt, sie auf
der Schulter lag, wir berührunglos
von der Brücke sahen. Ich erinnere mich
an das Gefühl, das deine Worte
bewirkten in mir. Es war gut.[8]

ALSO A LOVE POEM

I still know where we stood
It must have been about evening
I don't remember what you said to me
or I to you. I don't know
if I held your hand, lay
mine on your shoulder, we looked
without touching from the bridge.
I remember what your words
made me feel. It was good.

Parallels suggest that the precedent for this poem is Brecht's "Erinnerung an Marie A.," an earlier, frequently quoted poem about a half-forgotten encounter with a woman. The inflated rhetoric of Brecht's poem has been eliminated and with it the satiric edge. What remains, however, is an entirely plausible experience. Rathenow has written a sort of answer to the poem by Brecht, affirming the validity of feelings which the latter disparaged.

Finally, I would like to examine a poem sent to me by Rathenow shortly after his release from prison in early 1981:

DER HIMMEL IST NICHT TOT ER STIRBT . . .

mit jedem Knall des Düsenjägers. Kalt
liegen wir im Bett und schreien nicht
Die Vase umgekippt, der Blumenstrauß verdirbt daneben
dieser Brief von deinem Freund (jetzt Berlin-W.) und
der von meiner Freundin (sorry, es ist okay

Übermorgen gehts nach Spanien)

Du weißt, was ich weiß:
nicht aus, noch ein
Von deinen Lippen fällt es
Rot. Kein Blut. Nur Wein[9]

THE SKY IS NOT DEAD BUT DYING . . .

with every crack of the fighter plane. Cold,
we lie on the bed and don't scream
The vase turned over, the flowers ruined
Next to it this letter from your boy-friend (now West
    Berlin)
and that from my girl-friend (sorry, it's okay
In two days off for Spain)

You know what I know
It's not so fine
From your lips falls
red. Not blood. Just wine

The motion of the fighter plane might be said to represent the
dramatic turns in the policy of a highly armed state, the
reverberations of which are felt in the homes of its citizens.
Short poems usually tend to start with the concrete and move to
ever greater levels of abstraction. Here, on the contrary, the
movement is from a cosmic level to a political--and finally to a
domestic one. The development is simultaneously from a stanza
that is loosely organized and characterized by abrupt rhythmic

changes to a formal quatrain. This structure suggests an order which reasserts itself after cataclysmic upheavals. The gentler rhythm of the final stanza adds an element of calm to the message of foreboding.

In the eighties Rathenow has increasingly turned from the medium of poetry to the more public vehicle of drama. He has become known as a master of the grotesque, somewhat in the tradition of Kafka and of Polish surrealists such as Mrozek. The aggressiveness with which he satirizes contemporary bureaucracy has led many reviewers to neglect the more contemplative aspects of Rathenow's work. This is not the place to analyse his theatrical art in detail. Perhaps, however, Rathenow's poetry may direct people to a recognition that his work also has a gentler side.

CHAPTER XI

THE FAILED SYNTHESIS

In most of the East German poets we have looked at, a fundamental
tension has been observed. On the one hand, there is the tendency
to deny the existence of the individual, making men and women
interchangeable with one another. On the other hand, there is the
Romantic heritage, the exaltation of love and, by implication, of
the lovers. Put another way, the poets of the GDR have pursued a
paradoxical ideal: a sexual relationship that would be devoted
and faithful--yet anonymous. Such a possibility was suggested to
them by Marxist theory. The poets attempted to discover it in
practice. None of them, however, has managed to render it
convincingly.

Was this a creative tension or an unresolvable contradiction? It was at least creative in the sense that it
inspired the poets to write, producing some good material as a
sort of by-product of their experiments. Nevertheless, none of
the poets has even faced the problem directly. The older writers
such as Becher, Brecht, Wiens, Maurer and Kahlau simply refused
to recognize the contradiction. Mistaking their theoretical
constructions for authentic experience, they pretended to be both

personal and anonymous. The most successful of these was probably Maurer who, though unrealistic, was at least able to articulate an idyll of considerable beauty. But no progress toward a lasting synthesis was made.

As time went on, the tension grew more difficult to ignore. In Braun we find a poet who, unable to maintain even the pretense of a synthesis, swings dramatically from one extreme to another. The Romantic and collective ideals are found next to each other. But if the contradiction is artistically productive in his work, philosophically it is not. He has, despite an original style, no new ideas to offer. At times he chooses in favor of the collective ideal. Sometimes the selection is left open, but no real harmony between the two is ever achieved.

It is possible to see this unsuccessful attempt at synthesis as symtomatic of a larger disillusionment with the Communist experiment or at least its more extreme claims. Marxism was always a mixture of highly diverse ideas and traditions. Perhaps these have been held together far more by the dynamism of certain individuals than by any basic affinity. The Romanticism and desire for anonymity we have spoken of seem to be concrete manifestations of elements in the broader Marxist synthesis. These two tendencies correspond to the moralistic and mechanistic sides of Communism. People are appealed to in moral terms to struggle for the achievement of a Communist society. At the same time they are told that this ideal will be realized as the inevitable result of historical forces rather than by individual efforts.

In Kunert, older than Braun yet more contemporary, the entire prospect of resolving the contradiction has been abandoned. We are left with a quiet melancholy. In the poetry of Sarah Kirsch and Rathenow, we seem to have come full circle. There is not a great deal of love poetry written by the younger generation of the GDR. What is produced bears more resemblance to traditional love lyrics than to the ideological constructions of poets like Becher. In this, as in many other respects, East Germany may be said to have rejoined the mainstream of German literature.

Marxism has had a far stronger and more enduring hold over the imaginations of writers in the GDR than in other states of Central and Eastern Europe. Until about 1980 virtually all intellectual dissent in the GDR came from thinkers who spoke in the name of the Marxist tradition. Wolf Biermann, Robert Havemann and Rudolf Bahro are, perhaps, the most important examples. Marxism had strong indigenous roots in East Germany. Marx and Engels, after all, wrote in the German language and drew heavily on the philosophical traditions of German Idealism. Furthermore, the rise of Nazism seemed, in the decade after World War II, to have discredited other German traditions.

All of the authors we have discussed were at least strongly influenced by Marxist ideology. Their attitudes were largely formed by a confrontation with Communism, even when they ultimately rejected that view of the world.

The extent to which they thought in terms of Marxist categories and ideals has often isolated writers and intellectuals of the GDR from their counterparts in both Western and Eastern Europe. Influential philosophers such as Havemann and Bahro, for example, devoted an enormous amount of time and emotion to an intricate sort of utopian theorizing that is hardly understandable outside of a German context. For many of the youngest East German poets, however, Marxism is ceasing to be even a point of reference. Rather than following, rebelling against or trying to reform Marxist ideology, they are largely indifferent to it. They simply laugh at party decrees.

Two examples are the Berlin writers Bert Papenfuß[1] and Uwe Kolbe.[2] As the GDR emerges from its cultural isolation, these poets communicate a sense of excitement. Their poems constantly take off in unexpected directions, presenting new surprises in almost every line. The language of their love poetry, particularly that of Papenfuß, is tender but often deliberately casual. Kolbe, who has been influenced by such neo-Romantics as George and Rilke, sometimes mixes informal speech with a more elevated sort of diction. Neither of these poets shows any suggestion of a desire for anonymity. On the contrary, they delight in displaying all sorts of personal idiosyncracies. They tend to adopt charmingly eccentric sentence constructions and punctuation.

A poet who, almost two decades after her suicide in 1966 at the age of 41, has been receiving belated recognition is Inge Müller. During her own lifetime only a handful of her poems were published, in scattered journals and anthologies. Though her memory and reputation survived in literary circles, a full collection of her verse, entitled <u>Wenn ich schon sterben muß</u>, was not published until 1985. Much of her poetry describes the devastation of Germany at the end of World War II, often in terrifying detail. A refusal to adopt a tone of facile optimism after the war may have done much to delay her recognition, but this enables her work to strike a responsive chord today.

Müller is sometimes compared with Paul Celan, the great Jewish poet of the Holocaust. It is interesting to note, after so many decades, how similar the experiences of certain Germans and Jews can sometimes appear. No matter what the subject, Müller's poems are heavy with memories of destruction and premonitions of her own death.

She presents love as a tenuous bond between her and the world. The Romantic exaltation of love is not at all a matter of rhetorical flourishes. It is rather a realistic recognition that she needs love in order to survive. The desire for anonymity takes an even more concrete form--the temptation of suicide. Both are present in the following epigram:

LIEBE II

Da hängt ein Luftballon im Raum
Wie lang wird er da hängen
Die Schnur aus Draht hält ihn im Raum
Der Wind wird ihn wegdrängen.[3]

LOVE II

An air-balloon now hangs in space
But how long will it stay
A wire string holds it in place
The wind drags it away.

The balloon of love, as we know, was to break eventually. But if Inge Müller could not resolve the contradiction faced by GDR poets, the extent to which she confronted this gives power to her work. It will be interesting to note what other largely forgotten poets may be discovered as the early history of the Republic is reinterpreted.

It should be remembered, however, that the dilemma confronting the East German authors is by no means confined to the Marxist tradition. Laissez faire Capitalism, for example, also attempts to reconcile individual and collective aspirations, postulating a society in which the collective good results from each individual pursuing his own self-interest. The difficulty is a universal one, even if circumstances during the early history of the German Democratic Republic rendered it especially traumatic.

Precisely the universality of their concerns can sometimes render love poetry written in the early decades of the GDR moving, even in the absence of finer artistic qualities. Poetry has the ability to transcend even aesthetic considerations. This book is written out of a belief that every poet, regardless of how great or small his artistic skill, reveals much about his intimate beliefs and feelings in his verse. Though we cannot turn to it for consolation, a poor poem can be as touching as a great one. Indeed, a failed poetic endeavor of spectacular dimensions can have a special pathos. One thinks, for example, of the unfinished hymns of Hölderlin, in which the absence of certain words and lines has a poignant inevitability. The GDR poets under discussion may lack the stature of a Hölderlin. Most of them forfeit tragic grandeur by a complete inability to see their limitations. Nevertheless, their failures warrant at least a certain sympathy.

NOTES

Chapter I
The Romantic Heritage of Marxism
in East Germany

1 "Any Marxist theory of women's liberation must start at the level of general social theory, since it is impossible to get around the paucity of references in Marx's own work." Richard J. Evans, The Feminists: Women's Emancipation Movements in Europe, America and Australia 1840-1920 (New York: Barnes & Noble Books, 1977), p.185.

2 Evans, The Feminists, p. 155.

3 Leszek Kolakowski, Main Currents of Marxism: Vol. I, The Founders, translated, from the Polish by P. S. Falla (Oxford: Clarendon, 1978), p. 414.

4 Karl Marx, selection from Economic and Philosophic Manuscripts of 1844, translated from the German by Martin Milligan, in The Marx Engels Reader, edited by Robert C. Tucker (New York: W. W. Norton, 1978), p. 82.

5 Karl Marx, Economic and Philosophic Manuscripts, in The Marx Engels Reader, p. 83.

6 Karl Marx, selection from The German Ideology, translated from the German by W. Lough, in The Marx Engels Reader, pp. 159-160.

[7] Karl Marx and Friedrich Engels, Manifesto of the Communist Party, from the English edition of 1888, edited by Engels, no translator given, in The Marx Engels Reader, p. 488.

[8] Karl Marx, letter to Kugelmann, in Marx Engels Werke (Berlin: Dietz, 1965), Supplement #1, p. 535.

[9] Michael Löwy, "Marxism and Revolutionary Romanticism," in Telos, #49 (fall 1981), pp. 86-87.

[10] Edmund Wilson, To the Finland Station: A Study in the Writing and Acting of History (New York: Farrar, Straus & Giroux, 1972), pp. 134-135.

[11] Leonard P. Wessel, Karl Marx, Romantic Irony and the Proletariat: The Mythopoetic Origins of Marxism (Baton Rouge: Louisiana State University, 1979), p. 1.

[12] This has been noticed increasingly by scholars in the last decade or so. See, for example: Fritz J. Raddatz, Karl Marx: Der Mensch und seine Lehre (Munich: Wilhelm Heyne, 1975), p. 295.

[13] Karl Marx, "Menschenstoltz," quoted and translated in Wessel, Karl Marx, Romantic Irony, pp. 278-281.

[14] David Mclellan, Friedrich Engels, edited by Frank Kermode (New York: Viking, 1978), pp. 52-53.

[15] Friedrich Engels, The Origin of the Family and the State, revised version of a translation by Alec West, with introduction and notes by Eleanor Burke Leacock (New York: International Publishers, 1972), p. 128.

16 Engels, The Origin, p. 117.

17 Engels, The Origin, p. 132.

18 Engels, The Origin, p. 139.

19 Evans, The Feminists, p. 156.

20 Evans, The Feminists, p. 157.

21 "Yet the view of the radical feminists were in reality far removed from those of the Social Democrats, liberal individualism, not Marxian Socialism was their creed. The ultimate aim of the radical feminists was to secure self-determination for the individual woman." Richard J. Evans, The Feminist Movement in Germany 1894-1933 (London: Sage, 1976), p. 272.

22 Barbara Wolfe Jancar, Women under Communism (Baltimore: The Johns Hopkins University, 1978), p. 75.

23 Joan Landes, "Feminism and the Internationals," in Telos, #49 (fall 1981), p. 123.

24 Clara Zetkin, "Lenin on the Woman Question," appendix to Emancipation of Women: From the Writings of V. I. Lenin, with a preface by Nadezhda K. Krupskaya. No translator given (New York: International Publishers, 1972), p. 102.

25 Zetkin, "Lenin," p. 105.

[26] Zetkin, "Lenin," p. 104.

[27] Jancar, Women under Communism (Baltimore: Johns Hopkins University, 1978), p. 143.

[28] Kathy Vanovitch, "Innovation and Convention: Women in the GDR," in GDR Monitor, #2 (winter 1979), pp. 16-17.

[29] Alexander Stephan, "Johannes R. Becher and the Cultural Development in the GDR," in New German Critique, #1 (spring 1974), p. 84.

[30] Edith Georg, "Denkst du schon an die Liebe?," in Neue Deutsche Literatur, July 1977, p. 63.

[31] Sigrid Damm, "Tristan, Isolde und wir: Gespräch mit Günter de Bruyn," in Neue Deutsche Literatur, October 1978, p. 146.

[32] Heinz Czechowski, editor, Sieben Rosen hat der Strauch: Deutsche Liebesgedichte und Volkslieder von Walter von der Vogelweide bis zur Gegenwart (Halle/Saale: Mitteldeutscher, 1963), p. 6.

[33] Walter Lewerenz and Helmut Preißler, editors, Deutsche Liebesgedichte (Berlin: Neues Leben, 1963), p. 8.

Chapter II
Bertolt Brecht: The Extreme Reticence

1 Martin Esslin, Brecht: The Man and his Work (New York: W. W. Norton, 1971), p. 257.

2 Bertolt Brecht, "Erinnerung an Marie A.," in Deutsche Liebesgedichte, edited by W. Lewerenz and H. Preißler (Berlin: Neues Leben, 1963), pp. 264-266.

3 Hannah Arendt, "Profiles--What is permitted to Jove," in The New Yorker, November 5, 1966, p. 98.

4 Hans Kaufmann, "Brecht, die Entfremdung und die Liebe," in Weimarer Beiträge, January 1965, pp. 95-96.

5 Kaufmann, "Brecht," p. 96.

6 Bertolt Brecht, "Vom ertrunkenen Mädchen," in Gedichte, vol. 1 (Frankfurt: Suhrkamp, 1961), p. 53.

7 Brecht, "Vier Liebeslieder," in Deutsche Liebesgedichte, pp. 267-268.

8 Arendt, "Profiles," p. 70.

9 Klaus Schuhmann, "Späte Lyrik Brechts," in Weimarer Beiträge, Brecht Special Issue (Sonderheft) 1968, p. 48.

10 Kaufmann, "Brecht," pp. 100-101.

11 Kaufmann, "Brecht," p. 101.

Chapter III
Johannes R. Becher:
The Child Lost in Dreams

1 For an account of Becher's often troubled relationships
to the state, see: Alexander Stephan, "J.R. Becher and GDR
Cultural Development,"in New German Critique, #2 (1974), pp.
72-89.

2 Johannes R. Becher, "Liebe ohne Ruh," in Sieben Rosen
hat der Strauch: Deutsche Liebesgedichte und Volkslieder von
Walter von der Vogelweide bis zur Gegenwart, edited by Heinz
Czechowski (Halle/Saale: Mitteldeutscher, 1964), p.312.

3 Johannes R. Becher, "Von Liebe und Tod," in Deutsche
Liebesgedichte, edited by W. Lewerenz and H. Preißler (Berlin:
Neues Leben, 1963), p. 277.

4 Many commentators have remarked upon this. See, for
example: Konrad Franke, Die Literatur der Deutschen Demokratischen Republik (Munich: Kindler, 1971), p. 199. Also:
Hans-Dietrich Sander, Geschichte der schönen Literatur in der DDR
(Freiburg: Robach, 1972), p. 71.

5 Becher, "Du zeigst hinüber," in Deutsche Liebesgedichte,
p. 278.

Chapter IV

Paul Wiens and the "Weather-Vane of Love":
The Struggle for Artistic Autonomy

1 Paul Wiens, Beredte Welt (Berlin: Aufbau, 1953), pp. 125-127.

2 Paul Wiens, Nachrichten aus der dritten Welt (Berlin: Volk und Welt, 1957), pp. 34-35.

3 Schiller, "Kuba, Wiens: Über einige Probleme der neuesten deutschen Lyrik," in Weimarer Beiträge, Special Issue (Sonderheft) 1958, p. 83.

4 Wiens, Nachrichten, p. 35.

5 Schiller, "Kuba, Wiens," p. 90.

6 Schiller, "Kuba, Wiens," p. 90.

7 Schiller, "Kuba, Wiens," p. 90.

8 Fritz J. Raddatz, Traditionen und Tendenzen: Materialien zur Literatur der DDR (Frankfurt: Suhrkamp, 1972), p. 519.

9 Rainer Kirsch, "Kunst und Verantwortung: Probleme des Schifstellers der DDR," in Amt des Dichters (Rostock: Hinstorff, 1979), p. 29.

10 Paul Wiens, Dienstgeheimnis: Ein Nächtebuch (Berlin: Verlag der Nation, 1968), p. 5.

11 Reinhard Weisbach, "Die Sinnlichkeit der Ebenen oder die `kosmische Krankheit,' das Erdenweh: Paul Wiens und die literarische Gestaltung von Problemen der modernen Kosmologie" in Weimarer Beiträge, March 1969), pp. 545-560.

12 Paul Wiens, Vier Linien aus meiner Hand (Leipzig: Philipp Reclam jun., 1976), pp. 79-80.

Chapter V
Georg Maurer's "Figures of Love"
Escape into the Marxist Idyll

1 Georg Maurer, Gespräche (Halle/Saale: Mitteldeutscher, 1967), p.48.

2 Georg Maurer, "Dichtung und Wirklichkeit," in Der Dichter und seine Zeit (Berlin: Aufbau, 1956), pp. 147-156.

3 Dieter Schlenstedt, "Angst und Liebe im Werk Georg Maurers," in Weimarer Beiträge, May 1968, p.963.

4 Georg Maurer, "Gestalten der Liebe," in Gestalten der Liebe (Halle/Saale: Mitteldeutscher, 1965), p.103.

5 Maurer, "Gestalten," p. 105.

6 Leszek Kolakowski. Main Currents of Marxism: Vol. III. The Breakdown, translated from the Polish by P. S. Falla (Oxford: Clarendon, 1978), pp. 445-446.

7 Martin Walser, "Vom Tode von Ernst Bloch," in Tintenfisch/Jahrbuch: Deutsche Literatur, #14 (1978), p.46.

Chapter VI
Heinz Kahlau's DU:
The Denial of Individuality

1 Mathilde Dau, "Wege zum Publikum" (interview with Heinz Kahlau), in Auskünfte: Werkstattgespräche mit DDR Autoren, edited by A. Löffler (Berlin: Aufbau, 1974) pp. 252-253.

2 Heinz Kahlau, "Zueignung," in Du: Liebesgedichte (Berlin: Aufbau, 1976), p. 5.

3 Kahlau, "Ich liebe dich," in Du, p. 7.

4 Kahlau, "Die Liebe," in Du, p. 15

5 Kahlau, "Die Liebe muß sein!" in Du, p. 30.

6 Eva and Hans Kaufmann, Erwartung und Angebot: Studien zum gegenwärtigen Verhältnis von Literatur und Gesellschaft in der DDR (Berlin: Akademie, 1976), pp. 176-177.

7 Rudolf Dau, "Bauherrenprobleme (a review of Heinz Kahlau's Flugbrett für Engeln)," in Neu Deutsche Literatur, September 1976, p. 154.

[8] Kahlau, untitled poem, in <u>Du</u>, p. 74.

[9] Kahlau, untitled poem, in <u>Du</u>, p. 81.

Chapter VII
Günter Kunert's THE INNOCENCE OF NATURE:
The Use of Parody

[1] John Flores, Poetry in East Germany: Adjustments, Visions and Provocations (New Haven: Yale University, 1971), p. 281.

[2] Marcel Reich-Ranicki, Zur Literatur der GDR (Munich: Piper, 1974), p. 109.

[3] Lutz Rathenow, "Da sitzt einer und schreibt: Bemerkungen zu Günter Kunert's Werk--anläßlich keines Anlasses," in Neue Literatur: Zeitschrift der Sozialistischen Republik Rumänien, June 1979, pp. 85-87.

[4] Fritz J. Raddatz, Tradition und Tendenzen: Materialien zur Literatur der DDR (Frankfurt: Suhrkamp, 1972), p. 176.

[5] Flores, Poetry in East Germany, pp. 287-288.

[6] For the extremes to which Kunert's pessimism has gone in recent years, see: Fritz J. Raddatz, "I'd rather be dead than think the way Kunert does" (interview with Günter Kunert and Wolf Biermann), translated by David Caldwell in New German Critique, #23 (spring/summer 1981), pp.45-55.

7 Günter Kunert, "Laika," in East German Poetry, edited by Michael Hamburger (New York: E. P. Dutton, 1973), p. 88.

8 Flores, Poetry in East Germany, p. 288.

9 Rathenow, "Da sitzt einer," p. 89.

10 Günter Kunert, "Unschuld der Natur," in Unschuld der Natur: 52 Figurationen leibhafter Liebe (Berlin: Aufbau, 1968), p. 64.

11 Kunert, "Wir waren Zwei," in Unschuld, p. 24.

12 Flores, Poetry in East Germany, p. 280.

Chapter VIII
Volker Braun's "Liebesgedichte für Susanne M. in Flensburg": The Dialectical Passions

1 Hans Richter, "Fragt ihr uns oft genug?: Bemerkungen zu Volker Braun's 'Wir und nicht sie'," in Forum, #24 (1970), p. 18.

2 John Flores, Poetry in East Germany: Adjustments, Visions, and Provocations (New Haven: Yale University, 1971), p. 293.

3 Richter, "Fragt ihr," p. 19.

4 Volker Braun, "Liebesgedichte für Susanne M. in Flensburg," in Vorläufiges (Frankfurt: Suhrkamp, 1966), pp. 11-13.

5 Heinrich Heine, "Wenn ich in deine Augen seh," in Sieben Rosen hat der Strauch: Deutsche Liebesgedichte und Volkslieder von Walter von der Vogelweide bis zur Gegenwart, edited by Heinz Czechowski (Halle/Saale: Mitteldeutscher, 1964), p. 214.

6 Fritz J. Raddatz, Traditionen und Tendenzen: Materialien zur Literatur der DDR (Frankfurt: Suhrkamp, 1972) p. 183.

7 A highly acclaimed GDR novel offers a similar solution. After her lover has left for the West, the abandoned heroine finally learns to find solace in the life around her: Christa Wolf, Der geteilte Himmel (Berlin: Aufbau, 1963).

8 Volker Braun, Vorläufiges, p. 84.

9 Volker Braun, "Fastnachtsspaß" in Provokation für mich: Gedichte (Halle/Saale: Mitteldeutscher, 1967), p. 32.

10 One finds a similar melodrama in Volker Braun's remarkable novella entitled "Unvollendete Geschichte" where the impossibility of integrating sexual love into the framework of society is handled in a very radical manner. In Sinn und Form, May 1975, pp. 941-979.

11 From an unpublished interview with Volker Braun. Quoted in: Arrigo Subiotto, "The Lyric Poetry of Volker Braun," in GDR Monitor, #4 (winter 1980-1981), p. 11.

Chapter IX
Sarah Kirsch: A Feminine Perspective

1 For a discussion of Christa Wolf's relation to Feminism, see Alexander Stephan, "The Emancipation of Man: Christa Wolf as a Woman Writer," in GDR Monitor, #2 (winter 1979), pp. 23-30. In the eighties Christa Wolf has adopted a more overtly Feminist position. See, for example, Christa Wolf, Voraussetzung einer Erzählung: Kassandra (Darmstadt: Luchterhand, 1983).

2 Fritz J. Raddatz, Traditionen und Tendenzen: Materialien zur Literatur der DDR (Frankfurt: Suhrkamp, 1972), pp. 168-169

3 Sarah Kirsch, "Ein Gespräch mit Schülern," in Erklärung einiger Dinge (Ebenhausen: Langewiesche-Brandt, 1978), pp. 24.

4 Kirsch, "Gespräch," p. 22.

5 Kirsch, "Gespräch," p. 24.

6 Deutsche Liebesgedichte, edited Walter Lewerenz & Helmut Preißler (Berlin: Neues Leben, 1963), p. 346.

7 Quoted by Elke Erb in "Über Sarah Kirsch," afterword to: Kirsch, Erklärung, p. 69.

[8] One example of this is a book of monologues recorded by Sarah Kirsch in which women of various professions tell the stories of their lives: Sarah Kirsch, Die Pantherfrau: Fünf Frauen in der DDR (Reinbek: Rowohlt, 1978).

[9] Kathy Vanovich, "Innovation and Convention: Women in the GDR," in GDR Monitor, #2 (winter 1979), pp. 16-17.

[10] Women for Peace, "The Women's Letter," no translator given, in: John Sandford, The Sword and the Ploughshare: Autonomous Peace Initiatives in East Germany (London: Merlin/ END, 1983), p. 97.

[11] Hans-Dietrich Sander, "Literatur and Literaturpolitik," in DDR Handbuch, edited by the FRG Ministry for Inter-German Relations and under the direction of Hartmut Zimmermann (Cologne: Wissenschaft und Politik, 1985), p. 834.

[12] See: Christine Cosentino, "Literary Correlations between Sarah Kirsch's poem 'Der Rest des Fadens' and Elke Erb's Volume Der Faden der Geduld," in GDR Monitor, #5 (summer 1981), pp. 52-56. Costentino sees Sarah Kirsch's growing impatience with literary life in the GDR reflected in her poetry. In the subsequent issue of the same journal, Andy Hollis disputed Costentino's interpretations. This is not the place to undertake an analysis of their respective arguments. I will only say that I personally find Costentino's point of view convincing.

Chapter X
Lutz Rathenow: The Pattern Reversed

1 Georg Maurer, "Zur Deutschen Lyrik der Gegenwart," in Der Dichter und seine Zeit (Berlin: Aufbau, 1956) p. 58.

2 Hans-Dietrich Sander, Geschichte der schönen Literatur der DDR: ein Grundriß (Freiburg: Rombach, 1972), pp. 225-267.

3 Sander, Geschichte, p. 234.

4 Sander, Geschichte, p. 234.

5 Edmund Wilson has the following remarks on Marx's own use of imagery: "...if we isolate and examine these images, we can see through to the inner obsessions at the heart of the world-vision of Marx. Here all is cruel discomfort, rape, repression, mutilation and massacre, premature burial, the stalking of corpses, the vampire that lives on another's blood, life in death and death in life." To the Finland Station: A Study in the Writing and Acting of History (New York: Farrar, Straus & Giroux, 1972), p. 306.

6 Lutz Rathenow, "Entschuldigen Bitte," in Auswahl 78 Neue Lyrik Neue Namen, edited by Richard Pietraß, H. J. Schubert and W. Trampe (Berlin: Neues Leben, 1978), p. 118.

7 Lutz Rathenow, "Am Abend," in Neue Deutsche Literatur, February 1980, p. 108.

8 Lutz Rathenow, "Auch ein Liebesgedicht," in Neue Deutsche Literatur, February 1980, p. 108.

9 Lutz Rathenow, "Der Himmel ist nicht tot, er stirbt...," previously unpublished poem sent to the author of this book in 1981. The poem was later published in: Lutz Rathenow, Zangengeburt: Gedichte (Munich: Piper, 1982), p. 32.

Chapter XI
The Failed Synthesis

1 For an example of Papenfuß' love poetry, see: "erzaehl das mal keinem so naif," in Auswahl 78: Neue Lyrik Neue Namen, edited by Richard Pietraß, H. J. Schubert and W. Trampe. (Berlin: Neues Leben, 1978), pp. 104-105.

2 Kolbe has published a book of love poems: Uwe Kolbe, Abschiede und andere Liebesgedichte (Frankfurt: Suhrkamp, 1983).

3 Inge Müller, "Liebe II," in Wenn ich schon sterben muß: Gedichte (Berlin: Aufbau, 1985), p. 63

SELECTIVE BIBLIOGRAPHY

Arendt, Hannah. "Der Dichter Bertolt Brecht," in Die Neue Rundschau, January 1950, pp. 52-67.

----------"Profiles. What is Permitted to Jove," in The New Yorker. Nov. 5, 1966, pp. 68-111.

Auerbach, Thomas. "vom Kulturzirzkel in die Haftzelle des SSD." In Frankfurter Rundschau. Nov. 24, 1980. Reprinted as a flyer by Ullstein Verlag. No page number given.

Bathrick, David. "The Dialectics of Legitimation: Brecht in the GDR." In New German Critique, #2 (spring 1974), pp. 90-103.

Bebel, August. Die Frau und der Sozialismus (with a foreword by Eduard Bernstein). Berlin: Dietz, 1977.

Becher, Johannes R. Ausgewählte Dichtung: aus der Zeit der Verbannung 1933-1945. Berlin: Aufbau, no date given.

Becher, Lilly and Gert Prokop, eds. Johannes R. Becher: Bild-Chronik seines Lebens. With an essay by Bodo Uhse. Berlin: Aufbau, 1973.

Berger, Uwe and Günter Deicke, eds. Lyrik der DDR. Berlin: Aufbau, 1974.

Bloch, Ernst. Das Prinzip Hoffnung (Three volumes). Frankfurt: Suhrkamp, 1959.

Braun, Volker, Das unbezwungene Leben Kasts. Berlin: Aufbau, 1975.

----------Es genügt nicht die einfache Wahrheit: Notate. Suhrkamp, 1979.

----------Gedichte. Frankfurt: Suhrkamp Taschenbuch, 1979.

----------Gedichte. Leipzig: Philipp Reclam jun., 1979.

----------Vorläufiges. Frankfurt: Suhrkamp, 1966.

Brecht, Bertolt. Gedichte (in six volumes). Frankfurt: Suhrkamp, 1961.

----------Liebesgedichte. Edited by Elisabeth Hauptmann. Frankfurt: Insel, 1966.

Brettschneider, Werner. Zwischen literarischer Autonomie und Staatsdienst: Die Literatur in der DDR. Berlin: Erich Schmidt, 1972.

Cosentino, Christine. "Gedanken zur jüngsten DDR-Lyrik: Uwe Kolbe, Sascha Anderson und Lutz Rathenow." In The Germanic Review, LX/#3 (summer 1985), pp. 2-90.

----------"Literary correlations between Sarah Kirsch's poem 'Der Rest des Fadens' and Elke Erb's volume Der Faden der Geduld." In GDR Monitor, #5 (summer 1981), pp. 52-56.

----------"Volker Braun's Training des aufrechten Gangs: A Handbook of Poems for Party Members." In GDR Monitor, #6 (winter, 1981-82), pp. 31-39.

Czechowski, Heinz, ed. Sieben Rosen hat der Strauch: Deutsche Liebesgedichte und Volkslieder von Walter von der Vogelweide bis zur Gegenwart. Halle (Saale): Mitteldeutscher, 1964.

Damm, Sigrid. "Tristan, Isolde und wir: Gespräch mit Günter de Bruyn." In Neue Deutsche Literatur, October 1978, pp. 138-147.

Dau, Mathilde. "Exerzitien zum Thema Liebe" (Review of Kahlau's Du: Liebesgedichte). In Neue Deutsche Literatur, July 1972, pp. 140-141.

Dau, Rudolf. "Bauherrenprobleme" (Review of Kahlau's Flugbrett für Engeln) In Neue Deutsche Literatur, September 1976, pp. 154-156.

Demetz, Peter. Marx, Engels, and the Poets: Origins of Marxist Literary Criticism. Translated by from the German by Jeffrey L. Sammons. Chicago: University of Chicago, 1959.

----------Postwar German Literature: A Critical Introduction. New York: Schocken Books, 1970.

Drewitz, Ingeborg. "Der junge DDR-Autor Rathenow" In Der Tagesspiegel: Unabhängige Berliner Morgenzeitung. January 11, 1981, p. 25.

Empson, William. Seven Types of Ambiguity. New York: Meridan Books, 1955.

Endler, Adolf. "Fragt mich nicht wie: Zur Lyrik Inge Müllers." In Sinn und Form, February 1979, pp. 152-161.

Engels, Friedrich. The Origin of the Family, Private Property and the State. Revised version of a translation by Alec West. Edited with an introduction and notes by Eleanor Burke Leacock. New York: International Publishers, 1972.

Esslin, Martin. Brecht: The Man and his Work. New York: W. W. Norton, 1971.

Evans, Richard J. The Feminist Movement in Germany 1894-1933. Beverly Hills: Sage, 1976.

----------The Feminists: Women's Emancipation Movements in Europe, America and Australia 1840-1920. New York: Barnes & Noble, 1977.

Fischer, Louis. The Life of Lenin. New York: Harper & Row, 1964.

Fischer, Ruth. Stalin and German Communism: A Study in the Origins of the State Party. Cambridge: Harvard University, 1948.

Flores, John. Poetry in East Germany: Adjustments Visions and Provocations. New Haven: Yale University, 1971.

Franke, Konrad. Die Literatur der Deutschen Demokratischen Republik. Munich: Kindler, 1971.

Fühmann, Franz. Essays Gespräche Aufsätze 1964-1981. Rostock: Hinstorff, 1983

Geerdts, Hans Jürgen, ed. Literatur der DDR: in Einzeldarstellungen. Stuttgart: Alfred Kroener, 1972.

Georg, Edith. "Denkst du schon an die Liebe?: Frage an unsere Gegenwartsliteratur für Kinder." In Neue Deutsche Literatur, July 1977, pp. 63-77.

Gerber, Margy et al., eds. Studies in GDR Literature and Society 4. Lanham: University Press of America, 1984.

Gray, Ronald. Brecht: The Dramatist. New York: Cambridge University, 1976.

Grimm, Reinhold. Bertolt Brecht. Tübingen: Sammlung Metzler, 1961.

Gropp, Rugard Otto, et al. Ernst Blochs Revision des Marxismus: Kritische Auseinandersetzung Marxistischer Wissenschaftler mit der Blochschen Philosophie. Berlin: Deutscher Verlag der Wissenschaften, 1957.

Große, Anneliese and Reinhard Weisbach, eds. Weimarer Beiträge, Brecht Special Issue (Sonderheft) 1968.

Haase, Horst. "Heutige Welt aus lyrischer Sicht." In Neue Deutsche Literatur, January 1964, pp. 86-110.

----------"Interview mit Paul Wiens." In Weimarer Beiträge, March 1969, pp. 520-529.

----------"Die Sinnlichkeit der Ebenen oder die 'kosmische Krankheit,' das Erdenweh: Paul Wiens und die literarische Gestaltung von Problemen der modernen Kosmologie." In Weimarer Beiträge, March 1969, pp. 530-545.

Hamburger, Michael, ed. East German Poetry. New York: E. P. Dutton, 1973.

Hedlin, Irene Arten. The Individual in a New Society: A Study of Selected "Erzählungen" and "Kurzgeschichten" of the German Democratic Republic from 1965 to 1972. Bern: Peter Lang, 1977.

Heller, Peter. "Nihilist, into Activist: Two Phases in the Development of Bertolt Brecht." In The Germanic Review, XXVII/#2 (1953), pp. 144-155.

Hennig, Gerd. "Mass Cultural Activity in the GDR: On Cultural Politics in Bureaucratically Deformed Transitional Societies." Translated by Gunner Huettic. In New German Critique, #2 (spring 1974), pp. 38-57.

Huchinson, Peter. Literary Presentations of Divided Germany: The Development of a Central Theme in East German Fiction 1945-1970. New York: Cambridge University, 1977.

Huebener, Theodore. The Literature of East Germany. New York: Frederick Unger, 1970.

Jancar, Barbara Wolfe. Women under Communism. Baltimore: Johns
    Hopkins University, 1978.

Kahlau, Heinz. Du: Liebesgedichte. Berlin: Aufbau, 1976.

Kaufmann, Hans. "Brecht, die Entfremdung und die Liebe." In
    Weimarer Beiträge, January 1965, pp. 84-101.

Kaufmann, Hans and Eva. Erwartung und Angebot: Studien zum
    gegenwärtigen Verhältnis von Literatur und Gesellschaft in
    der DDR. Berlin: Akademie, 1976.

Kelling, Hans-Wilheim. The Idolatry of Poetic Genius in German
    Goethe Criticism. Bern: Herbert Lang, 1970.

Kirsch, Rainer. Amt des Dichters. Rostock: Hinstorff, 1979.

Kirsch, Sarah. Erklärung einiger Dinge. Ebenhausen, Langewiesche-
    Brandt, 1978.

----------Katzenkopfpflaster: Gedichte. Ebenhausen,
    Langewiesche-Brandt, 1978.

----------Die Pantherfrau: Fünf Frauen in der DDR. Reinbek:
    Rowohlt, 1978.

----------Rückenwind. Ebenhausen: Langewiesche-Brandt, 1977.

Klussmann, Paul Gerhard and Heinrich Mohr, eds. Jahrbuch zur
    Literatur in der DDR/Band III. Bonn: Bouvier, 1982.

Kolakowski, Leszek. Main Currents of Marxism: Its Rise, Growth and Disillusion (3 volumes). Translated from the Polish by P. S. Falla. Oxford: Clarendon, 1978.

Kolbe, Uwe. Abschiede und andere Liebesgedichte. Frankfurt: Suhrkamp, 1983.

Kunert, Günter, ed. Dimension. Special DDR issue 1973.

----------Unschuld der Natur: 52 Figurationen leibhafter Liebe. With drawings by Fritz Cremer. Berlin: Aufbau, 1968.

----------Verkündigung des Wetters: Gedichte. Munich: Carl Hanser, 1966.

Kunze, Reiner. The Wonderful Years. Translated from the German by Joachim Neugroschel. New York: George Braziller, 1976.

Landes, Joan. "Feminism and the Internationals." In Telos, #49 (fall 1981), pp. 117-126.

Lang, Ernst. DDR und Deutschlandforschung in der Bundesrepublik Deutschland einschließlich Berlin (West). Bonn: Gesamtdeutsches Institut, 1984.

Laschen, Gregor, ed. Lyrik aus der DDR. Zürich: Benziger, 1973.

Legters, Lyman H., ed. The German Democratic Republic: A Developed Socialist Society. Boulder: Westview, 1978.

Lenin, V.I. The Emancipation of Women. No editors or translators given. Preface by Nadezhda K. Krupskaya. With an appendix entitled "Lenin on the Women Question," by Clara Zetkin. New York: International Publishers, 1972.

Löffler, Anneliese. ed. Auskünfte: Werkstattgespräche mit DDR Autoren. Berlin: Aufbau, 1974.

Love, Myra. "Christa Wolf on Feminism: Breaking the Patriarchal Connection." In New German Critique, #16 (winter 1979), pp. 31-53.

Löwy, Michael. "Marxism and Revolutionary Romanticism." In Telos, #49 (fall 1981), pp. 83-95.

---------- "Jewish Messianism and Libertarian Utopia in Central Europe." Translated by Renee B. Larrier. In New German Critique, #20 (spring/summer 1980), pp. 105-115.

Luxemburg, Rosa. The Letters of Rosa Luxemburg. No translator given. Edited with an introduction by Steven Eric Bronner. Foreword by Henry Pachter. Boulder: Westview, 1978.

Marx, Karl and Friedrich Engels. The Marx-Engels Reader. Edited by Robert C. Tucker. New York: W. W. Norton, 1978.

----------Werke (33 volumes with 2 supplements). Berlin: Dietz, 1965.

Marx, Karl, Friedrich Engels and V.I. Lenin. Über die Frau und die Familie: Auswahlband. Leipzig: Verlag für die Frau, 1976.

Maurer, Georg. *Essay I*. Halle (Saale): Mitteldeutscher, 1968.

----------*Der Dichter und seine Zeit: Essays und Kritiken*. Berlin: Aufbau, 1956.

----------*Gedichte*. Halle (Saale): Mitteldeutscher, 1964.

----------*Lob der Venus*. Berlin: Verlag der Nation, 1961.

Mclellan, David. *Friedrich Engels*. Edited by Frank Kermode. New York: Viking, 1978.

Millet, Kate. *Sexual Politics*. Garden City: Doubleday, 1970.

Mittenzwei, Werner. *Brechts Verhältnis zur Tradition*. Berlin: Akademie, 1972.

Morley, Michael. *Brecht: A Study*. London: Heinemann, 1977.

Müller, Inge. *Wenn ich schon sterben muß: Gedichte*. Berlin: Aufbau, 1985.

Pietraß, Richard, H. J. Schubert and W. Trampe, eds. *Auswahl 78: Neue Lyrik neue Namen*. Berlin: Neues Leben, 1978.

Raddatz, Fritz J. "I'd Rather Be Dead Than Think the Way Kunert Does." Interview with Günter Kunert and Wolf Biermann. Translated from the German by David Caldwell. In *New German Critique*, #23 (spring/ summer 1981), pp. 45-55.

----------Karl Marx: Der Mensch und seine Lehre. Hamburg: Hoffman & Campe, 1977.

----------Traditionen und Tendenzen: Materialien zur Literatur der DDR. Frankfurt: Suhrkamp, 1972.

Rathenow, Lutz. Boden 411: Stücke zum Lesen und Texte zum Spielen. Munich: Piper, 1984.

----------Contacts/Kontakte: Poems and Writings by Lutz Rathenow. Translated by Boria Sax. Providence: The Poet's Press, 1985.

----------"Da sizt einer und schreibt: Bemerkungen zu Günter Kunerts Werk--anläßlich keines Anlasses." In Neue Literatur: Zeitschrift des Schriftstellerverbands der sozialistischen Republik Rumänien, June 1979, pp. 83-90.

----------"Luftholen." Poems in Neue Deutsche Literatur, February 1980, pp. 106-113.

----------Mit dem Schlimmsten wurde schon gerechnet: Prosa. Frankfurt: Ullstein, 1980.

----------Zangengeburt: Gedichte. Munich: Piper, 1982.

Reich-Ranicki, Marcel. Zur Literatur der DDR. Munich: Piper, 1974.

Richter, Hans. "Fragt ihr uns oft genug?: Bemerkungen zu Volker Brauns 'Wir und nicht sie'." In Forum, #24 (1970), pp. 20-25.

Sander, Hans-Dietrich. Geschichte der schönen Literatur in der DDR: Ein Grundriß. Freiburg: Rombach, 1972.

----------"Literatur und Literaturpolitik." In DDR Handbuch. Edited by the FRG Ministry of Inter-German Relations and under the direction of Hartmut Zimmermann. Cologne: Wissenschaft und Kunst, 1985, pp. 830-842.

Sandford, John. The Sword and the Ploughshare: Autonomous Peace Initiatives in East Germany. London: Merlin/END, 1983.

Sargent, Lydia, ed. Women and Revolution: A Discussion of the Unhappy Marriage of Marxism and Feminism. Boston: South End, 1981.

Sax, Boria. "The East German Peace Movement." In Cross Currents, XXXII/#4 (winter 1982), pp. 388-394.

----------"East German Writers and the State." In Index on Censorship. II/#4 (1982), pp. 33-35.

Schiller, Dieter, "Kuba, Wiens. Über einige Probleme der neuesten deutschen Lyrik. In Weimarer Beiträge, Special Issue (Sonderheft) 1955, pp. 75-94.

Schlenstedt, Dieter. "Angst und Liebe im Werk Georg Maurers." In Weimarer Beiträge, May 1969, pp. 962-975.

Schteck, Joachim, ed. Saison für Lyrik: Neue Gedichte von siebzehn Autoren. Berlin: Aufbau, 1968.

Schuhmann, Klaus. Der Lyriker Bertolt Brecht 1913-1933. Munich: Deutscher Taschenbuch, 1971.

Smith, Duncan. "Peter Hacks and Volker Braun: Two views of Classicism and Marxist Orthodoxy." In GDR Monitor, #4 (winter 1980-81), pp. 14-21.

Sodaro, Michael J. "Limits to Dissent in the GDR:Fragmentation, Co-optation and Repression." In Dissent in Eastern Europe. Edited by Jane Curry. New York: Praeger, 1983, pp. 82-116.

Steineckert, Gisela. Brevier für Verliebte. Berlin: Neues Leben, 1976.

Stephan, Alexander. "J. R. Becher and GDR Cultural Development." Translated by Sara and Frank Lennox. In New German Critique, #2 (spring 1974), pp. 72-89.

----------"The Emancipation of Man. Christa Wolf as a Woman Writer." In GDR Monitor, #2 (winter 1979-80), pp. 23-29.

Subiotto, Arrigo. "The Lyric Poetry of Volker Braun." In GDR Monitor, #4 (winter 1980-81), pp. 1-13.

Vanovitch, Kathy. "Innovation and Convention: Women in the GDR." In GDR Monitor, #2 (winter 1979-80), pp. 15-22.

Walser, Martin. "Vom Tode von Ernst Bloch." In Tintenfisch/ Jahrbuch: Deutsche Literatur, #14 (1978), pp. 46-48.

Weisbach, Reinhard. "Die Sinnlichkeit der Ebenen oder die 'Kosmische Krankheit,' das Erdenweh." In Weimarer Beiträge, March 1969, pp. 545-560.

Wessel, Leonard P. Jr. Karl Marx, Romantic Irony and the Proletariat: The Mythopoetic Origins of Marxism. Baton Rouge: Louisiana State University, 1979.

Wesson, Robert G. Why Marxism: The Continuing Success of a Failed Theory. New York: Basic Books, 1976.

Wiens, Paul. Beredte Welt. Berlin: Aufbau, 1953.

----------Dienstgeheimnis: Ein Nächtebuch. Berlin: Verlag der Nation, 1968.

----------Nachrichten aus der dritten Welt. Berlin: Verlag der Nation, 1968.

----------Vier Linien aus meiner Hand: Gedichte 1943-1971. Leipzig: Philipp Reclam jun., 1971.

Wilson, Edmund. To the Finland Station: A Study in the Writing and Acting of History. New York: Farrar, Straus & Giroux, 1972.

Witt, Hubert, ed. Erinnerungen an Brecht. Leipzig: Philipp Reclam jun., 1966.

Wolf, Christa. Der geteilte Himmel. Berlin: Aufbau, 1963.

----------Voraussetzung einer Erzählung: Kassandra. Darmstadt:
    Luchterhand, 1983.

Wolff, Lutz W., ed. Frauen der DDR. Munich: Deutscher
    Taschenbuch, 1976.

INDEX

DDR-Literatur im Tauwetter

von Richard A. Zipser

unter Mitarbeit von Karl-Heinz Schoeps

Band I und II:	**Wandel – Wunsch – Wirklichkeit**	656 S. $ 84.-
Band III:	**Stellungnahmen**	191 S. $ 34.-
		alle drei Bände $ 115.-

Das vorliegende dreibändige Werk gibt einen Einblick in die Literatur der Deutschen Demokratischen Republik von 1971 bis 1978 und dokumentiert dabei vor allem die kulturpolitische Tauwetterphase von 1971 bis 1976.

Der Inhalt der drei Bände umfasst literarische Werke (Kurzgeschichten, Gedichte, Aufsätze, etc.) von 45 Autoren, Interviews, kritische Berichte und biographisch-bibliographische Notizen.

Eine Einführung informiert über wichtige literarische Entwicklungen und Tendenzen in der DDR seit 1945.

Aus dem Inhalt

In Band I und II werden 45 Schriftsteller aus der DDR durch Textproben, die zumeist in der Tauwetterphase 1971–1976 entstanden sind, durch biobibliographische Angaben und Autorenbild vorgestellt. Die Autoren äussern sich selbst zu der Frage nach dem Ziel ihrer literarischen Arbeit.

Band III enthält Interviews mit 37 Autoren aus der DDR, die sich zumeist während der Tauwetterphase 1971–1976 zu persönlichen, literarischen und kulturpolitischen Fragen äussern wie: Worin liegt die Funktion der Literatur und Kunst im sozialistischen Staat? Welchen Einfluss haben die Erfahrungen Ihrer Jugend auf Ihr Werk gehabt? Welchen Unterschied sehen Sie zwischen der DDR-Literatur der siebziger und der vorangegangenen Jahre? Welche Besonderheiten hat die Literatur der DDR innerhalb des deutschen Sprachraumes? Welche Rolle sollte die Literatur in der heutigen Gesellschaft spielen?

VERLAG PETER LANG AG

Jupiterstraße 15, CH-3015 Bern

PETER LANG PUBLISHING, INC.

62 West 45th Street, USA – New York, NY 10036